$250K
CONSULTING

Double or triple your income – start a consulting company!
How to ramp up fast, survive the first year, pull in paying
clients, gain trust, and avoid breaking the unwritten rules

Bill Yarberry, CPA

Bill Yarberry, CPA

CONTENTS

Bill Yarberry, CPA

THE PARADOX OF INDEPENDENT CONSULTING

W hat is more risky than independent consulting? Answer: just about every job in the marketplace. In this book I'll show you how a core set of soft and hard skills, techniques, attitudes, and processes combine to ensure your success as an independent consultant. It seems paradoxical. A business created out of thin air, with no guaranteed income, benefits, or office support develops into a healthy and reliable money making machine that:

- Provides significantly more income than what you would earn from traditional employers.
- Protects you from the massive technological disruptions that will continue for the foreseeable future.
- Presents a continuous flow of skill-expanding challenges.
- Ensures that no single mistake or bad relationship with a powerful individual derails your career.
- Reduces (partially) the impact of all the "isms"—racism, sexism, ageism, etc.

The traditional career path may offer good compensation, benefits, and a defined progression—as long as you work at that company. What it does not provide is protection against layoffs, poor profits (destroying your bonus), personal vendettas, required relocations, travel requirements, and possible isolation if you are no longer on the promotion track. Some futurists suggest that the deep changes sparked by artificial intelligence may eliminate white- and blue-collar jobs faster than new ones are created, at least in the short run.

If there is any one single insight that I've had over the past fifteen years as an independent consultant it is this—consultants rarely fail due to poor subject-matter competence. Mostly they fail by breaking the unwritten rules. My intent in this book is to shine a light on both the written and unwritten rules of engagement. "XYZ Corp" will never be your client. It may say that on paper, but your real client is, for example,

Sally. She gave permission for you to start. She has explicit business needs and your job is to satisfy them. But under the surface, she and every other client have self-esteem and status-recognition needs as well. Success is about meeting both visible and hidden requirements. None of this eliminates the need for ethical and legal good behavior; it simply means that you must always be aware of the forces that drive human behavior.

Do you have the right stuff?

The short answer is yes. You have the right stuff. If you've worked in a complex environment, set goals, can work with other people, learn quickly, complete projects, and plan your work, then you can do this. To help you decide:

- Talk to people who have worked as independent consultants. They can give you a sense of the day-to-day pressures, what it took for them to ramp up, and how they see their ongoing prospects.
- Consider going to boot camp with the big firms if you need a segue into starting your own business. You may not get the sense of what it takes to be independent using this approach, but you will see multiple approaches to sales, project management, politics of large organizations as well as the pace of work typically required of "big 4" (or however many there are in your specialty) consultants. When you're working for the big firms your main job is to make money for the partners, so whatever else they say, sales is what they mean. This can be good training. It's possible that you will enjoy the work and thrive, but most people—let's say 98%—do not become partners and move to other jobs once they get enough experience. My work with PricewaterhouseCoopers was a great learning experience, but in retrospect it was not essential to success. Go with large consulting firms if you need to, but do it with eyes wide open.
- Think about your tolerance for risk. As we'll discuss later, your personal financial strength certainly influences how easy it is to take the leap, but the risk is not particularly high for someone absolutely determined to make it as an independent consultant. The first six to twelve months may be considered the school of hard knocks, but it's ruthlessly effective for self-learning. You'll find out what you're good at, how potential paying customers see you, what skills matter most, and your capacity for running projects while marketing

at the same time. The ancient philosopher Socrates said, "Know thyself." Easy to say; hard to do.

- As the lawyers are fond of saying, "notwithstanding the above ..." all you *have to have* is a DBA (doing business as), a FBN (fictitious business name in California) or even the minimalist approach of using your own name. Go for it!
- It's a great way to make a living

Why consulting? There's no guaranteed pay or benefits and an uncertain future. Why do so many professionals choose independent consulting as their primary source of income? I hope by the end of this book you'll see that if you're willing to work, learn, and recognize the importance of soft skills, independent consulting provides benefits that you can't get anywhere else. Four benefits immediately come to mind.

First, there's the money. According to the Census Bureau, in 2015 the top 5% of American households earned $214,462 per year and the top 1% earned $465,626. Once established, independent consultants can easily find a position at the top 5% or above[1]. My peak yearly income was just shy of $300,000.

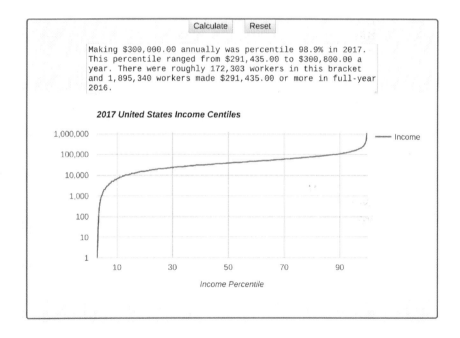

---

[1]Lake, Rebecca. "How Much Income Puts You in the Top 1%, 5%, 10%?" *Investopedia*, 15 Sept. 2016, www.investopedia.com/news/how-much-income-puts-you-top-1-5-10/.

Income Distribution in 2017[2]
Courtesy "Don't Quit Your Day Job ..." https://dqydj.com

You can charge by the hour, by the day, or by the project. For example, I charged one of my larger clients $50K for a two-month project, with a rate of $150/hr for any work past the expected two-month duration. In discussions with my peers it was clear that rates of $80 to $300 per hour are certainly possible, with even higher rates if you judge right and charge by the project. A side benefit is that because you are never completely certain when the next check will come in, you'll delay your personal spending as a safety precaution. Then when the payment comes in (and sometimes you get two checks at once), it seems like the cash gods are smiling on you. Since you can't count on regular income, in the long run your consulting practice forces personal financial discipline and makes you cash rich.

Second, consulting has a built-in psychological shield. You will never have to say "I got fired." Yes, you might lose a client but that's just business. Unlike terminations (voluntary or involuntary), losing a client is merely a learning experience. Besides, successful consultants will sooner or later lose all their clients—that's the nature of the business. But then, of course, you often get them back when the need arises.

Third, your family and social peers will be impressed. There's a certain prestige that goes with moderate risk taking to create a new business and the personal wealth that goes with it.

Finally, you'll enjoy the sheer excitement of doing new things, acquiring new skills, and associating with other successful professionals. When I started ICCM Consulting, I had in mind the phrase "Internal Controls and Cost Management." It was fortunate that I used an acronym because over time my projects evolved far beyond the original plan. Consider keeping your company name as generic and nonspecific as possible—you don't want to spend $5K on a marketing/branding effort, only to discover later that you are more successful in an unrelated business sector or technology.

There's one more benefit that comes to mind: the commute. Some days it is zero, depending on the client and the project. Working from your home office could cut one to two hours from your workday.

---

[2] "Income Percentile Calculator for the United States. What Percent Are You?" *DQYDJ*, 5 Feb. 2018, dqydj.com/income-percentile-calculator/.

GETTING STARTED: BACK-OF-THE-ENVELOPE PLANNING

Can I do this?

For many people considering independent consulting, the first consideration is immediate cash flow after quitting their day job. Think of it as a question of priming the pump. How do I get from day zero to day 120 or 180 when my first honest-to-goodness check comes in the mail?

There's no universal answer to that question. My first year as an independent consultant netted around $10,000. The second year brought in $50,000, the third year was several multiples of the second year, and within ten years my annual ICCM income was just shy of $300,000. I had some rather intense moments of doubt the first year. I had chosen to focus my practice on telecommunications cost management, which was my job at PricewaterhouseCoopers and part of my job at a pipeline company. After about eighteen months I realized that selling telecom savings projects was a hard task, at least for me, so I switched in midstream to audit support consulting. I wish I could tell you that it was the result of careful strategic planning but it wasn't—by chance I talked with the VP of Internal Audit for a manufacturing company in Houston. He said he wanted expertise for SOX (Sarbanes-Oxley regulation) work but didn't want to pay Big 4 rates. Sarbanes-Oxley, particularly in its early years, was a boon to consultants and auditors everywhere. It was inspired by the high profile collapse of Enron and some other large firms in the early 2000s. It forced a major revamp of the internal control/accounting systems for many firms.

What kept me and my family floating for those first scary years was a combination of drastic expense scale-back, savings, and the perception that opportunities were opening. So upfront funding is most likely the reason many otherwise-qualified people do not start their own consulting business. My recommendation is to:

- Cut your living expenses to the bone while you still have your day job. At this point in your business life, you must have low debt, cash on hand, and the ability to borrow funds for your business. Plan to stay on a "war footing" for twelve to twenty-four months. Can you iron your own shirts or blouses? Cut back on dining out? That's the kind of thinking you need to do before starting your business.
- Avoid treating personal or even business expenses as sacred cows. This means, for example, your first branding package would be a basic set of business cards, logo, etc. from a website like fiverr.com rather than from a $1,000+ higher end marketing service. If you know someone in the branding business you may get a starter package at a cut rate. At the same time, spreading business around to those who might refer you is prudent.
- Reserve your credit for the business rather than personal expenses. Accept in advance the reality that the check from your first client will take forever to get to you. I did not have a problem with my first check; however, I had a problem with another client whose project manager set up my firm with the wrong internal code. As a result, my client's accounts payable system sat on the invoice for several months. I ultimately got the funds but it felt like I was the mark at the carnival who never finds the pea under the shell.

Why your clients need you

Why do companies, nonprofits, and government agencies bring in consultants? One reason is the business world's constant downsizing. You don't hear much about companies going on a hiring spree. That's because there's almost a universal belief in the practice of reducing workforce while increasing output. Whether it's done by outsourcing or layoffs, the process never stops until lurching adjustments are required to continue doing business. It's difficult to fine-tune this process. Sometimes staff is cut too much and efficiency gains cannot be ramped up quickly enough to meet production goals. So one of the first avenues of business for the independent consultant is as a specialized fill-in. There's nothing wrong with getting business that way because it gives you an opportunity to sell by simply being there.

Another factor that affects the demand for independent consultants is the lack of fungibility that exists for complex work in the marketplace. The classic example of a fungible employee is an assembly-line worker. For complex work, however, the people who are left over after a layoff may not be able to efficiently execute the projects that the terminated employees were working on. So here again, you are available with the right skill set to either manage or provide expertise for the project.

Expertise is another issue but it may not be a single skill that makes the difference. Independent consultants may have a bundle of skills, perhaps not all equally strong, but good enough to meet the client's requirements. So perhaps the client needs one fourth of a project manager, one-fourth of a financial analyst, and half a strategist. It's hard to bring in a fourth of a person, so one of the advantages that the independent consultant typically brings to the table is a broader range of skills. It simplifies life.

This may not sound like a particularly exciting prospect, but sometimes you get work by being a throwaway resource. Organizations don't always know what they want to do. They try things. Sometimes they work and sometimes they don't. Bringing in an outsider makes it easier to ramp up an experimental project and shut it down if it doesn't work or is unprofitable. One of my associates told me of a department in one firm that laid off thirty employees and brought twenty-eight of them back as contractors. From your perspective, it's facetime. Later we'll discuss the distinct role of management versus consulting. The consultant need only worry about her process and quality of deliverables. She does not make the final decision and is not responsible for the outcome; that's management's job.

Although companies, especially large companies, are often presented in the media as being heartless, that's not completely true. Many of the managers and employees within the business do consider the welfare of others. They generally do not like to hire and fire based on short-term needs. Many times reasonable and responsible managers will delay hiring resources until it's completely obvious that there's a long-term need. Meanwhile the independent consultant is available to fill the gap.

Finally, if you've been in your industry awhile, you can provide your client with a perspective on what other organizations are doing. You don't need to reveal confidential client information, but you can certainly present trends and approaches for specific problems. For example, in the IT world the methodology to develop systems is always an item of interest. Some firms use a traditional systems-development lifecycle; others use rapid prototype methods. It can be useful to a CIO, for example, to know what methods are in general use.

Money needs, today and tomorrow

According to The Houston Chronicle[3], the average 2017 national rate for consulting work was $97,000. This number is based on voluntary completion of surveys so, from a statistical perspective, it is biased because it is not truly random. I suspect that this number is skewed toward the low end because the high earners do not have time to fill out a survey. It is also lowered by the inclusion of consultants working for consulting firms. Most independent consultants I know in the Houston area earn more than that and a few considerably more. $250K per year is at the high end of consulting income but is certainly attainable.

You can become wealthy (not overnight, of course) through independent consulting. To keep your earnings at the highest levels, you'll need to periodically sustain long hours of work and/or scale your business by using subcontractors. Projects come at irregular intervals. If you are currently engaged on a full-time project and you have a good relationship with your current client, ask if you can spend a day or two a week with another client. It may even be beneficial to your original client; there is typically downtime in any project where you are waiting for the client to provide some information. Rather than burn hours in less-productive activities, work on your new project while you wait.

Success requires you to maintain life basics in good order. Nothing is an "unalloyed good"—there's a cost to everything—and consulting is no exception. To maximize income, you'll need to streamline the rest of your life. Exercise, sleep enough, eat veggies, keep peace in your family. The anger of Achilles in the Iliad makes for great literature but serves poorly as base for personal productivity. Manage your core life skills successfully and the benefit will show up in your professional life and income stream. Health tracks productivity.

Paycheck to paycheck

You may be an outstanding saver, you may be diligent in claiming every possible tax deduction, but the first year in business you'll feel like a paycheck-to-paycheck person. The ramp-up period is simply part of paying your dues. Because it takes time to start up the consulting cash machine, you may find yourself doing a lot of short-term thinking. Can my car go another couple of months without an oil change? Does it make sense for me to mow my own grass? Can the family skip the vacation this year? It makes a big difference to your mental state and reduces anxiety if you know

---

[3] "Independent Consultant Salary." Accessed February 5, 2018. http://work.chron.com/independent-consultant-salary-1613.html.

these questions are going to come up. You can plan, anticipate, and communicate these expectations with your friends and family. If you are fortunate, you'll be able to line up work before you leave your day job and the transition will be much easier.

Getting through the first year

So how exactly do you get through the first year? Of course, you'll need to cut personal expenses. Even for the business, it is important to distinguish between essential expenditures such as taking prospective clients out to lunch, and higher risk expenditures such as radio advertising. In the first year, or at least until the checks start arriving, you need to manage cash with extreme care.

There are many cuts in your personal expenses that will not hurt you in one year of downsizing, after which you can return to your normal lifestyle. As you look over these possibilities, remember that you only must get past the first year. Overall, you'll earn more as an independent than as an employee. A few example cost cuts include:

- Review every service you use, such as lawn care, professional dry cleaning, and car washes. Nothing is cheaper than DIY. Of course, after your business is firmly established, your time will be too valuable for tasks that can easily be transferred to others.
- Cut subscriptions except for professional journals or other highly relevant publications.
- Review your insurance rates. Raising your deductible may help your cash flow without substantially increasing risk.
- Review small but repeating charges to your credit card. For example, for years I paid $15 a month for a business class efax service. After reviewing my charges and thinking about whether I had really benefited from the service, I stopped it. Although people still use fax, it is not the essential commutation tool it once was.
- Reduce the number of times per week you dine out.
- Buy used. Ebay and Amazon-used are good options.
- Read books on the thrifty lifestyle. Some of the recommendations are extreme but most are worth considering. Of course, do not neglect healthcare.

Avoid loans if you can. A line of credit may help you minimize expenses by doling out cash only as needed; there's no large cash balance in the bank to give you a false sense of security. Much of your success as an independent consultant relates to mind space — new ideas, approaches, research, and skill acquisition need to occupy your mind every day. If you are stressed about loan payments coming due, it will be that much more difficult to develop new business. Also, keep a line of credit available to initially fund travel expenses before the client reimburses you. On one engagement I had to fund a subcontractor's Houston-Miami air flights and other out-of-pocket expenses up front. The client paid me at ninety days on the nose, but I had some anxiety for a while.

Getting through the first year is an exercise in optimism and caution at the same time. Positive thoughts keep your output strong. Caution is needed to make your initial cash cushion last as long as possible.

Avoid apples served up by snakes

Now let's talk about where you'll be a year or two down the road. Sometimes cash will flow. Other times it gushes. You feel like a cash junkie; life is wonderful. This is exactly the time when you need to put your ultraconservative financial hat on, because some time down the road you will have a revenue gap. It is coming; it happens to all of us. We just don't know when. For example, in 2008 the results of the subprime mortgage defaults began to feel rather personal. My anchor client nearly went bankrupt and I was worried that my services would no longer be needed. As a desperate measure, I volunteered to lower my rates by 20% (it pays to be seen as a team player). After a few months the client stabilized and I was able to increase my rates back to the previous level.

So, don't be tempted during the good times to neglect your strategic reserve. The snake (high cash-flow periods) will entice you to eat the apple (your reserve). Don't. Being financially conservative is the price of independence.

GETTING STARTED: THE MECHANICS

Many books have been written on the relative merits of legal/tax structures. Options include sole proprietorships, subchapter S, C Corp, LLC, DBA ("doing business as"), and simply working under your own name. I'm not a lawyer, so I will not offer much advice here. But think about this—the form your business takes is not frozen in time, and you can always change as your business grows. In one short-lived company, I went through the hassle of setting up a C corp. It may be cool to have an official seal and stock certificate paper, but believe me, it's not worth it unless you have some specific reason. What is important is to get started. It is perfectly legal to work under your own name although it is probably best to at least file as a DBA ("Doing Business As") at your local courthouse. I started my business by registering "ICCM Consulting" as my DBA and a few years later filed with the Texas Secretary of State as "ICCM Consulting, LLC." An hour online and $500 later I was officially in business. In California DBAs are called "Fictitious Business Names." An LLC gives you some additional legal protection. As an example, see Wikihow's write-up at http://www.wikihow.com/Create-a-DBA-in-Texas. The only exception to this simplicity is the change from an LP or LLC to a corporation. A corporate legal structure is overkill for most consultancies.

The following is an excerpt from a *Houston Chronicle* article (http://smallbusiness.chron.com/file-doing-business-as-2322.html):

"Business owners that do not want to use their own name can file an Assumed Name Certificate with the secretary of state's office or the county clerk's office to create a 'Doing Business As' or fictitious business name. This name may be used to conduct business transactions that include opening business bank accounts and credit accounts, and filing state and federal tax returns or to promote the business using the name on marketing materials, websites and other media."

Ideally, you should engage an attorney to set up your business, particularly if it is a partnership or more complex than a sole proprietor business. Consider options to set up an SEP IRA[4]. Also, consider the possibility that your work may change direction. Do not make the name overly narrow. Use a PO box so that you don't need to go through the inconvenience of changing addresses once your clients have you set up in their accounts payable systems. You cannot simply start submitting invoices with a new address. Most organizations today carefully control vendor setup, including address changes.

If your business grows so much that you need to hire employees, great. Just be aware that your record keeping, taxes, and reporting requirements increase dramatically when you hire the first employee. For a small business it is often easier to outsource payroll to a service provider like ADP than to do it yourself. There could be penalties if you do payroll/reporting incorrectly. On the other hand, using independent contractor help is far simpler—order the forms (free) from the IRS and send out 1099s at calendar year end. No quarterly taxes to pay, no other forms, etc. If your 1099 worker is not familiar with the details of this relationship, explain it thoroughly. Repeat to them several times: a) you are not an employee and have no rights to employee benefits, and b) you must file and pay your own taxes out of your earnings – nothing is being held back from your check.

Power tools

If there were a gold standard for professional tool kits, then yours should surpass it. The best tools make you better, faster, and smarter. They include software, hardware, standard meeting practices, big data analytics, a plethora of Web applications, mobile apps, and sometimes just having two pens in a meeting so you can lend one out. Some of the items below will be obvious, but there's always that one or two that could be improved on. Also, the pace of technology is such that as-yet-unheard-of algorithms will regularly show up in the marketplace. Here is a short list:

- A powerful calendaring system that crosses all your devices, provides alerts, creates invites, helps tag photos, and provides other functionality.

---

[4] A Simplified Employee Pension (SEP) plan provides business owners with a simplified method to contribute toward their employees' retirement as well as their own retirement savings. Contributions are made to an Individual Retirement Account or Annuity (IRA) set up for each plan participant (a SEP-IRA).

- The most recent version of MS Office; alternatives include Google Docs and LaTex, both of which are free. LaTex has a longer learning curve but can produce polished, professional looking documents. You may want to have a combination of text tools.
- Contact software, such as Google Contacts. Use it a lot, for both personal and business. It should be your repository for not just basic name, address, etc., but should also include notes, such as "called John Smith on 3/24/16 regarding an analysis of payables. He said ..."
- Flowcharting software (Visio or open source). Its use varies by industry.
- Mind-mapping application (iMap from Tony Buzan or one of the many free ones available).
- Templates of all kinds: proposals, reports, contracts, invoices, stationery with your logo and PO box address.
- A standard billing process. There may be some value in more elaborate systems but I find Excel spreadsheets work fine if the process is consistent. Just be sure you can always break down your billable work for the client, using whatever structure is required—by project, charge code, etc. If your business grows and becomes more complex, consider double entry accounting software, such as Quick Books. I never found Quick Books necessary for ICCM Consulting but every consulting practice has its own requirements, particularly if substantial, depreciable assets are part of the business. Always keep records with sufficient backup – envision an IRS auditor looking over your shoulder.
- Prewritten text to respond to emails asking about your services. Of course, make sure the response matches the query. Otherwise, you will compromise your firm's image as a highly responsive and high touch customer service consultancy. Compare the charm of a "warm, responsive, and customer first" culture with the "cold, snobbish and impersonal" image carried by some of the larger firms.
- Nonconfidential samples of work product.
- A global, unstructured data application, such as Evernote or OneNote, to keep research, miscellaneous ideas, critical emails, and other information to be searched. The best nuggets of information come in randomly, and you need a strong retrieval system to find it after a few months have passed.
- Short and long bio for ready inclusion in speaker lists, proposals, even Amazon's author central.
- Voice-to-text system. Use Dragon Naturally Speaking to generate a rough first draft of a lengthy report or simply to makes notes at the end of the day. It's a big time saver. One note of caution—spend the time to train the system to your voice and feed it samples of your writing. That will improve accuracy.

Note that Windows and Google Docs also have voice-to-text features, with no additional costs.

Home office

The IRS has specific rules related to the home office business deduction. If you are going to take the deduction, of course pay attention to the detailed requirements, such as the use of the office for business purposes only. However, in the larger scheme of things it's more important that you configure your home office to give you the maximum output and maximum responsiveness to your clients. Don't contort your office simply to take a deduction that may be small relative to your business income. For the auto mileage deduction you can still consider your home as your business office, even if you do not specifically take the home office deduction. See a CPA or get one of the many business tax consumer-level books on the market. Before any of this, make a conscious decision about using a home office or leasing space for a business office. Unless you intend to bring clients to your office or have employees, an outside office is a costly option that will likely not pay for itself, and you must furnish it, pay for Internet access, phone, parking, etc. In some cases, family or living arrangements may interfere with the working at home option; high noise, interruptions or even sales people knocking on the door. Office Sharing services such as www.wework.com offer a cheaper and often better equipped work environment, without the financial commitment of a traditional rented office. Again, avoid the posh sites until you are regularly profitable (in the twelve to twenty-four month range).

In the previous section we talked about tools; they go hand in hand with your home office. You need to constantly think about not just how you do things but how you do them with maximum efficiency. That affects the physical layout of your office. For example, you shouldn't use a computer desk that requires you to stop what you're doing to stand up for document scanning. A wraparound desk is more efficient. Your landline telephone needs to be handy; your supplies close and organized, and the acoustics need to match your personality/working habits. For example, I have a 150-year-old wall clock whose ticking somehow puts me in a more-focused working state, while for others it would be a complete distraction. Some people work best listening to hard rock or indie guitar riff. Find out what helps you concentrate and put that in your office, whether it's classical music or even the android service you can now get to play ambient Starbucks noise. The home office list is pretty long, but here are a few things that come to mind:

- An ergonomic chair. Spend a lot of time selecting the right chair; it has an outsized effect on your energy level. It's a completely personal decision. For example, I use an old banker's chair rather than some of the exotic models you can find on the Internet.
- The standard office objects that have been around for a long time, such as staplers, highlighters, various colored pens, and large paper pads for brainstorming. Sometimes when you need to think broadly and creatively it's good to get away from the computer. Look at paper instead of pixels. Humans have been drawing, using eye-hand-brain coordination, for a lot longer than they've been using MS Office.
- A powerful, fast desktop PC.
- The highest quality monitor you can afford.
- A landline phone system that has a good full-duplex speaker and other features that help you keep track of calls' duration, etc. There may be times when a cell phone is just not good enough. A headset can be helpful if you find yourself on the phone while looking up information on your computer.
- Record calls if you have clients who talk faster than you can possibly take notes. I use the free app Call Recorder Pro on my cell phone.
- Install a separate land line solely for business. Change the ringer tone so that you know it is your business line, make sure the answering machine (or service) mentions your company, and ask for callback information. Avoid lengthy voicemail instructions; they annoy most people. Use the Internet to find examples of efficient and business-like voicemail messages.
- A door. We all care for our families/roommates/friends and need to spend time with them. However, it's not a clever idea to commingle personal and business matters during the day. You'll wind up doing neither one very well. A shut door indicates you need privacy for your work.
- The fastest Internet connection you can buy in your neighborhood.
- A small filing cabinet for those documents that cannot be stored as scanned or electronic images (e.g., your passport).
- Positioning of keyboard, mouse, and desk so that your hands and arms are not strained.
- A powerful and easy-to-use backup system for local and cloud storage. Google Drive is free and simple to use. I used a combination of cloud, a 0.5 TB thumb drive kept on my keychain and several large external USB 3.0 drives. My fear of data loss also impels me to make a 100% backup on an external USB drive which is the disconnected from the PC. This "air wall" method ensures that lightning will not run through my home computer network and destroy everything attached. I'll at least have my data, no later than one month old.

- An accurate voice-to-text system. I use Dragon Naturally Speaking. Google's free voice typing app is getting better each year.
- Lighting appropriate for you.
- A large tablet, Kindle, Nook, etc. Use a larger screen when reading electronic books and magazines. As of this writing you can get a Kindle Fire for $50, so you could have one next to your office easy chair and another for reference when traveling.
- A timer if you must work for hours on a heads-down project. A 3-5 minute break every thirty minutes will improve your productivity. See https://tomato-timer.com/ for a convenient, free Internet timer (see "pomodoro technique").

Pricing your services

Many larger consulting firms will charge their customers at a rate nearly double what the individual doing the work is paid. You can typically underbid those firms by charging 70-75% of their rate. For example, at the time of this writing one Houston firm charges $135 per hour for higher-end financial services work. The professionals doing the work are paid around $65 per hour. In that situation you could, for example, charge $95 per hour and still be a bargain to the client. Some prospective clients will take advantage of this knowledge and offer close to the $65. Others will be more concerned about getting a quality product and establishing a reliable source of expertise. In my experience, most clients are not going to arm wrestle you to get a bottom dollar rate. Always allow $5/hour as a bargaining chip, something you can throw in if a procurement manager needs to show his prowess by getting the fees down. It happened to me once.

Low cost is generally best until you have a base of clients and a strong consulting record. The buyer must justify to her boss why she brought in a sole proprietor (read: risky) consultant rather than a larger firm. Larger firms are perceived as more reliable and stable, correctly or not; their resources are at least theoretically fungible. The buyer is not stuck if something happens to the resource.

Some clients are reluctant to provide enough detail for you to assess the number of hours required. In that case you can provide minimum and maximum figures, based on your current understanding of the project. I'm sure there are firms out there that will take advantage of an inexperienced consultant; so far, I have not run into any. Of course, there will be some who ask for a presentation then use the ideas in-house. In my early days of consulting I brought a large tax savings opportunity in front of a technology manufacturing company in Austin. They had not considered the idea, then said thanks and gave the project to someone else. Sometimes the story changes in the middle of the project and it takes twice as long to finish as initially thought. If you have communicated well with the client, the reasons for higher-than-expected invoices should be clear.

The following is an example of pricing for one engagement (dollars are real, name has been changed):

Resource	Hourly Rate	Minimum Estimate for Project	Maximum Estimate for Project	Minimum Estimated Fees	Maximum Estimated Fees
John Doe, Principal Consultant	$130	500 Hours	650 Hours	$65,000	$84,500
Other Technical Resources	$125	15 Hours	30 Hours	$1,875	$3,750
Total		515 Hours	680 Hours	$66,875	$88,250

Boilerplate

If you are in the business long enough you begin to think the contents of your disk drive are worth more than you are. The accumulation of successful proposals, contracts, executive reports, and other documents improves your output in every way—speed, quality, and responsiveness. At the beginning of your practice acquiring a robust set of templates is almost as important as getting your first client. Templates fall into two categories:

- Business documents related to acquiring, contracting, communicating with, and billing the client. These are your "plumbing" templates.
- Work-related templates that help you deliver the end product. For example, when providing IT Audit work to clients I used a structured spreadsheet of

key controls for Sarbanes-Oxley compliance. The content changed to some extent from client to client, but the structure was fixed.

Your sales-related templates (e.g., PowerPoint presentations) need to be kept evergreen. For these types of documents you should peruse sites such as slideshare.com, Garr Reynolds' site[5], canva.com or fiverr.com to obtain the most dazzling graphic presentations. But for other, more prosaic documents, cosmetic evergreening is not expected. The following are templates that you'll want to have handy on your hard drive for maximum responsiveness to the client:

- Short and long bios
- Contracts
- Cover page and introduction to a proposal
- Engagement letter
- Quick blurb/elevator speech—what do you do? What are your focus areas?
- Letters of recommendation
- Logo and company graphic art
- Nondisclosure agreements
- Presentations of all sorts
- Progress reports
- Proposals and statements of work
- Publications list
- Marketing trifold (less important now than in the past)
- Work programs and check-off lists
- Examples of frequently requested spreadsheets. For example, you may be in a business that uses six sigma for quality control. Graphs, statistical reports, and so on can typically be modified quickly from one client to the next. Unless you are in the graphic arts or publications business itself, there is no need to be original. Inspiring ideas permeate the Internet.

Corporate bullies

People arrive at independent consulting in many ways. A few are fortunate enough to start in their early twenties. Most come from the ranks of big-company employees. Unfortunately, large companies are increasingly forcing employees to sign noncompete contracts, sometimes with onerous terms. According to a 2/3/16 *Wall Street Journal* article written by Aruina Viswanatha, "non-compete agreements— common in computing and engineering jobs, where proprietary technology can be at stake—are spreading to other industries and stretching further down the corporate

---

[5] Reynolds, Garr. "Top Ten Slide Tips." *Garr Reynolds Official Site*, www.garrreynolds.com/preso-tips/design/.

ladder. Labor law experts say some employers appear to be using them to prevent turnover among rookie employees they have spent time and money training. Since the agreements are private contracts, they generally are enforced through lawsuits." From a discussion with one of my peers in California, I understand that her state has strong laws protecting individuals from work choice harassment from large corporations.

Legal advice is beyond the scope of this book, but here are some general points to keep in mind:

It is not likely that the noncompete clauses can be enforced if they prevent you from making a living in your chosen field. Noncompete restrictions typically include a one-to-two-year limit. After that you're free to approach clients of your former employer. Occasionally a firm with a bully mentality will try to make your life miserable. If that happens you may want to consult an attorney. Nobody has the right to stop your business simply because you might interfere with their revenue stream at some vague point in the future. Honor the specific terms of your contract, but fight if the harassment continues.

Contingency projects

Some consulting boutiques earn their living by obtaining a cut of savings identified through analyzing duplicate payments, IT costs, transportation bills, telecommunications charges, and other expenses. It is certainly a legitimate business model. My recommendation is for you to think a long time before committing to this approach. Following are some pros and cons:

Pros:

- The client does not risk dollars up front—nothing is owed if you don't identify savings, so the sale is theoretically easier because the up-front risk is reduced.
- If a large savings opportunity is identified you could earn substantial fees, sometimes with relatively little work.
- Finding verified, hard-dollar savings is a reputational asset that boosts future sales opportunities.
- As you repeat the same types of engagements, your expertise and efficiency grow exponentially. You can also better estimate up front whether the cost-savings opportunities are worth the effort.

Cons:

- You can alienate some individuals in your client's organization. For example, suppose you find a remote office that uses a specific hardware infrastructure configuration to support their telecommunications traffic. You analyze usage of the hardware and circuits, finding that utilization is close to zero. As a result, the client can drop one of the circuits, avoiding hundreds of dollars a month. Here is the rub: although it is unfair, the CIO or even CFO may say to the telecom manager, "If ABC consulting can come in here and find this level of savings after a few days' work, then what were *you* doing all this time?" This happens a lot in contingency work. Make every effort to remind client management that you work as a specialist, with a narrow perspective (for this project) and with only one task—save money. It is easier for you to find savings than it is for the telecom manager; he has dozens of tasks every day and you have one.
- You may not find significant cost reductions, e.g., a unified (covering all subsidiaries) accounts payable department with up-to-date duplicate pay detection will usually be less profitable for you than an organization with multiple accounts payable systems and poor payment controls. For example, a well-controlled accounts payable department will have a three-way match for payments control—the invoice, the purchase order, and receiving report must all match.
- You could win the battle and lose the war. Example: after three weeks work, you identify $700,000 in duplicate payments and claim 30% as your fee. That works out to a compensation of $70,000 per week. The client pays per contract. However, all the client remembers is how embarrassed they were to tell management that you identified $700,000 in savings but they had to pay out $210,000 in fees. People resent anything that looks like easy money. Never mind that you took years to develop the skills to find the savings. It's all about appearance and some fuzzy sense of "fairness."
- Your income could have dramatic swings over time, especially if you're new to the game. Contingency work requires a large initial bank balance.
- There's a degree of routine and sameness in most contingency work. It is narrow and perhaps boring. Do you wear the same color shirt or blouse every day? Do you vary your diet from day to day? People differ significantly in their tolerance for routine. Only you can judge your suitability for contingency work.
- Lower level employees can torpedo your project if they resent you being there. One of my high school friends, president of a top ship safety inspection company in Houston, invited me to look for cost savings on a contingency basis. Even with his sponsorship, the project went nowhere. The telecom

manager and staff resented anyone looking into their business. After countless delayed requests for information, I had to fold.

- Finally, getting paid for contingency work can be messy. The client could say, "I already had the item on my scheduled to do list, so it doesn't count as a new discovery." It could turn into an ugly dispute. Contingency work at best is a tense business environment.

For some individuals and consulting practices contingency works well. My recommendation is to match that business model to your strengths, weaknesses, and preferences. It is rather like being an actuary—you either are one or are not one. Being a little bit of an actuary or a little bit of a contingency practitioner does not work.

Taxes

I'm not a tax accountant so any advice here is general; see your tax pro for the definitive answers. Nonetheless, I'll venture a few suggestions:

- Whatever you do, don't skip quarterly payments. You may find yourself in an argument with the IRS because they don't seem to understand that your income stream is irregular. If your business earns $200K this year they are looking for you to pay taxes on $50K of revenue every quarter. If you instead pay according to what you actually earned each quarter, you'll sometimes be fined a few dollars. It is unfair, but you have to determine if it's worth your time to protest.
- Keep particularly good records for your business. For example, in some circumstances the auto mileage between your home office and client is a deductible business expense, but you need to keep detailed records (personal versus business use) to support it.
- Document the purpose/client for business lunches.
- Run business expenses and revenues through a separate business checking account. The same applies to business versus personal credit cards.
- Send out 1099s for your subcontractors on time.
- Don't feel obligated to file on April 15. If you need to delay filing, file an extension and complete your return when you don't have to cut into billable hours.

Insurance

Most of your clients will expect you to have professional liability insurance. Expect the process to be somewhat bureaucratic. Your larger clients will have requirements that sometimes are not applicable, so be sure and review the details carefully. For example, I had a security review project with a large firm that required its vendors to carry special insurance for chemical accidents. Some of its vendors carry dangerous chemicals from one location to another. I successfully argued with the company's administrators that there was nothing in my work that even remotely involved chemicals, so I was able to get that requirement dropped and saved several hundred per month.

There have been less than 100 people killed in terrorist attacks against the United States since 9/11. Not to lessen the impact of these terrible crimes, note that statistically speaking, out of 300 million people the likelihood of your company suffering from a terrorist attack is vanishingly small. Decline terrorist insurance unless your client insists on it.

The price you'll pay for insurance varies considerably. As an example, in 2014 my sole proprietor company paid $2,602 for twelve months of professional liability coverage. Be sure to keep all paperwork related to your various insurance policies because you'll be asked by some clients to provide information related to your auto insurance. You may also be asked to obtain a "designation of covered persons' document" from your auto insurance company. Your client may want to be listed on your professional liability insurance coverage.

Things you do not need right now

A BMW is cool. I used to have one myself. But you are fooling yourself if you justify it as a business necessity. Clients will not award you business because they like your car. So, particularly in the early years of your practice, avoid burning through your cash because of a perceived need for prestige. There are many examples of what you don't need:

- High-end luxury cars.
- Designer briefcases—they don't get noticed as much as you think.
- Extraordinarily expensive wardrobe—Walmart clothes won't do but $5K Armani suits or a Sentaler camel coat are more about a need to impress than any business requirement.
- Two-hundred-year-old handwoven rugs from Persia.

- Extended warranties (why would a company sell something to you if there's no profit in it?).
- High-rent office space, particularly if customers will not be coming to your office. Good service typically means you go to the client's office.

These are all nice artifacts to have when your practice has matured and you no longer have a going-concern risk. Just don't convince yourself they are for the business. That being said, don't carry thrifty to such an extreme that you look desperate or impoverished. Even a clean pickup truck with a bashed in fender makes the potential client question whether you are a success oriented person.

Bill Yarberry, CPA

MARKETING

A draft business plan is the best plan

WHY IS A DRAFT BUSINESS plan better than a polished plan? There are a couple of reasons. Number one, unless you're going for a loan, you'll never get the value out of a polished, perfect presentation. Your marketing business plan is for you and anyone that you would care to have look at it. The second and more important reason is that a perfected plan implies a static plan. That's probably the worst sin a new consultant can make. Your business planning and marketing needs to be nimble, adjustable, and continually modified to fit your clients, industry, and location.

Push/pull

You can acquire clients by pushing out your message, attracting them through good work and reputation or both. Which approach is best for you depends on your personality, marketing budget, specialty, and any number of other factors.

Broad-stroke marketing to potential buyers

There are any number of channels you can use to get in front of potential buyers:
- Send an introductory email. Keep it short, provide some useful information, and list your contact information. Mailing list services such as InforUSA, Direct Mail, and Vistaprint provide a targeted audience you can use as a

starting point. Of course, your email response rate will be much less than 1% but your message may hit the inbox of a potential buyer at just the right time.

- Mail hard-copy letters, brochures, and postcards. Physical mail seems antiquated and is certainly expensive; however, there is less competition in the paper world than in cyberspace. All you need is a list of potential buyers (names, titles, and addresses), MS Word for mail merge, and good-quality envelopes and paper. Sometimes a handwritten address gets attention in a stack of mail. A few years ago I sent out 400 letters, got two responses, and one new client. Your time and the expense limit this approach.
- Buy radio talk-show time. A thirty-second ad reaching a million listeners might cost $2-$4K. You'll need to arrange for production of the ad (voice-overs, etc.) but there are plenty of firms ready to help. If your specialty is narrow, radio might not be a good use of your marketing dollars.
- Find groups in LinkedIn that match your areas of expertise and tastefully source out business opportunities. You'll need to be a good citizen on the site, providing information and contacts to others, in order to get the full benefit of participation. Writing a short (less than 1,000 words) article or business opinion piece for Linkedin can also improve your visibility.
- Advertise in the trade rags if the economics make sense for your business.
- Make cold calls (and yes, for most people the high rejection rate is hard to take). I made cold calls one bleak winter morning. That was the end of my cold-call marketing. Cold calling, even for the those good at it, results in a small percentage of successes. It is also time consuming. If you are one of those rare individuals who can pull it off, do so. There are other ways to market for the rest of us.

As in gas mileage, your results may vary. Direct marketing can be time consuming, expensive, and distracting if you already have a full workload. Some consultants are successful with this technique because of their extroverted personality. They draw energy from conversations, talking about the business, calling to follow up, speaking, and milling about whenever the opportunity arises. These are all excellent ways to get business. However, you may lean more toward the introverted/deep-subject-matter end of the spectrum. If so, pace yourself so you don't run out of psychic energy. Always make friends and do things for other business people to build relationships. Reciprocity matters.

Your email list

One of the best ways to sell is to let potential clients know what you're thinking, reading, and doing. As you acquire an email database, use it to deliver information on a "news you can use basis." Long-term, you could use a marketing tool such as

MailChimp or Constant Contact. With these tools you can maintain statistics and avoid spam filters once your mailing list becomes large. Of course, when you're dealing with an individual client for anything other than FYI then use your direct business email.

The following list of features/functions, courtesy of http://email-marketing-service-review.toptenreviews.com/, shows what you can expect from the leading vendors:

Contact Management:

- Dashboard Ease of Use
- Import Mailing List
- Remove Unsubscribed Contacts
- Group Email Contacts
- Automatically Detect Duplicate Emails
- Require Opt-in
- Social Media Tools
- Demographic Segmentation
- Account Health Meter

Email Creation:

- Dashboard Ease of Use
- Import Mailing List
- Remove Unsubscribed Contacts
- Group Email Contacts
- Automatically Detect Duplicate Emails
- Require Opt-in
- Social Media Tools
- Demographic Segmentation
- Account Health Meter

Create a gravitational pull

I prefer to *attract* clients. It sounds obvious but it is one approach of several. It is different from the heavy-marketing, "*push* method." Ninety-five percent of my business comes from word-of-mouth or potential clients who know me from professional organizations or have read my articles and books. Consider yourself as the sun in a solar system, where planets and asteroids are drawn into your gravitational field. It is the best and most reliable way to thrive in the complex consulting world of the twenty-first century. Some ways to create pull include:

- Make yourself visible at meetings of professional organizations, preferably those with a high percentage of potential buyers. For example, my early days in consulting included IT Audit projects and analytics. Of the two most relevant organizations—The Institute of Internal Auditors (IIA) and Information Systems Audit and Control Association—I favored the IIA because of the higher percentage of Fortune 500 audit executives who attend.

- Volunteer for positions at professional and charitable organizations. Although you have to be careful with your time, all forms of circulation add to your visibility. The jury is still out on whether groups specifically targeted to leads will generate new business. I found networking groups were more oriented toward small business, salespeople working on commission, etc. In contrast, professional groups, focused on member education and sharing experiences, usually include people in positions of greater responsibility. Use judgment and watch your time commitments.

- Speak as often as you can. Don't worry about being a great speaker. Not everyone is funny and entertaining. Unless you're an entertainment consultant, your skills need merely be of the "workhorse" type. If you present your subject matter well, keep the needs of the audience in mind, and finish on time, that's enough. And please, do not bore your audience with more than fifteen seconds of talk about your own business.

- Write professional articles. Do not confuse fiction writing with nonfiction. Fiction is hard to do well and only a tiny percentage of those doing it make serious money. Nonfiction, on the other hand, is much easier to break into. You need to know your topic; avoid long, boring passages; and submit your promised material on time. There are thousands of trade and professional magazines. Editors are constantly on the lookout for new material and will typically be happy to publish factual, relevant articles. Keep in mind that every person was once a novice in their subject area, so publishing "obvious" material is certainly an option.

- Write books. Book writing is a longer-term effort but is well worth the effort. You can choose to either publish via traditional publishers such as John Wiley or Prentice Hall or you can go the independent route and work through Amazon Kindle or Smashwords. If you're writing a book to support and build your consulting practice, then your primary concern is not the money directly earned from book sales; instead, what matters is the enhancement of your professional image. With self-publishing you can certainly earn a higher percentage of sales, but even today there is a perception that traditionally published books are a cut above those that are self-published. This is primarily due to the lack of a filtering mechanism in the self-published world, whereas big-name, traditional publishers will not typically put out a book that does not meet certain standards. Just make sure that your keep your primary objective in mind. For example, when writing this book, I wanted to provide others with an antidote to the usual "look at my Ferrari and million dollar fees" boasting seen in the self-help lecture circuit. Over time I have become annoyed with this self-serving elitism. My original title for this book was "Consulting for the Rest of Us."

One of your core objectives should be to ask the question, "How can I help people in general and potential clients specifically?" It's a matter of perspective. Think— what knowledge, actions, services, and contacts do I have to help the client? But even if the client needs services outside your skill set, listen carefully. Anything you can do to facilitate solutions to problems helps your business immensely. Knowing reliable providers in multiple fields outside your own is a plus for you. Don't look bored when your client or potential client talks about a problem that you can't solve. These are the kinds of client-centered notes that you should record at the end of the day. The more thoroughly you understand his needs, whether in your specialty or not, the more likely you are to come up with a solution or at least broker a solution. Besides, referring your client to someone unrelated to your services makes it more likely that you will get referrals from others in turn.

Business development

"All happy families resemble one another; each unhappy family is unhappy in its own way"
Leo Tolstoy, *Anna Karenina*

How to sell? Answer: Think shotgun—use every trick in the book. Personal contacts, emails, article writing, blogs, Twitter, website, running clubs, and professional associations all work. The uncertainty and randomness of sales is a barrier to consulting success. The shotgun analogy is apt because you never know in advance which sales channels will work. When asked about education the economist John Kenneth Galbraith remarked, "Sometimes important things are done inefficiently, but still need to be done." That applies to sales as well. You have no choice but to work tirelessly, through every means possible, to get in front of potential clients. The majority of your effort will be like cast iron deer on the lawn of useful marketing—completely wasted. It is the successful 2%, often from left field, that pays for all the rest. Wouldn't it be nice if we knew the 2% in advance?

Since sales is the major pain point of getting your business started, I will repeat the message: clients come in randomly. Your anxiety may be off the charts. After so much effort, no nibbles are on the line. How can you stand it? I can't reduce your pain but I can tell you that the business will come in some form if you market enough and go through diverse channels. It is all about *velocity* – the faster you run in marketing, the more potential customers will see you.

A side benefit of your initial, intense sales effort is that it concentrates the mind. What do you offer that clients want? Can you describe the end result if they bring you in? Can you outline the five or ten reasons why you are better than your peers? Do you have a story or an elevator speech ready?

On the front end of your business, the pressure is intense. How you respond to that stress will impact your success. During times of little work, you have to double down on every channel that gets you in front of potential clients. Phone calls, emails, lunches, professional meetings, and even charity events keep you in circulation. Randomness rules. Your first clients will most likely come from an offhand conversation or a brief meeting somewhere. In the old days merchants would typically invest in multiple ship voyages because of routine losses at sea. It is impossible to know which of your ships will come through, so you have to invest in all of them.

New clients

How to keep the pipeline full? There is no simple answer, no simple set of rules to develop your customer portfolio. Like Leo Tolstoy's happy families, successful business development includes common good practices. Failed consultancies go off track in different ways. The following are proven steps for acquiring new clients:

- Spend most of your business development time with potential buyers rather than your peers. It is easy to feel busy meeting with people you already know. Are they buyers?

- Understand degrees of separation. You have a circle of friends and associates that you know directly. They are separated from you by degree one. Those individuals, in turn, have friends and associates that you may not know or know only slightly—the second degree of separation. Mark Granovetter, a professor of sociology at Stanford, has popularized this concept, naming it "the strength of weak ties." According to Granovetter, if you are looking for new business or a job, it is not your immediate associates (degree of separation of one) but your weaker connections, such as separation degrees two or three, that are most valuable. Think of it this way—you've probably already run through all the opportunities known to your close friends, but there are many more opportunities (numerically) in the weaker ties. Weak ties grow exponentially as you move away from your immediate circle of friends and associates.

- Use every opportunity to teach. You may not get paid much (or zero). That's OK because it is part of your marketing velocity. I taught for a few semesters at Le Tourneau night school and made some useful contacts for later work. My practice eventually grew to the point that I couldn't afford the time to teach, but it was particularly useful in the early days.

- Write a blog. WordPress simplifies the technical steps to get started. All you need to do is keep adding fresh material so that readers and potential customers have a reason to revisit your site.

- Use Starbucks as your meet-and-greet locale for short meetings. Sometimes your prospects are so busy they don't have time for lunch at a restaurant, but they may be able to talk to you from 7:30 to 7:45 a.m. over coffee. Busy people don't like to navigate to new locations,, so stick with well-known places like Starbucks so you can focus on business, not decor. You should avoid Starbucks with constant high traffic, noise and shortages of workspace.

- Write in a notebook (or dictate into your mobile phone using voice to text) anything important after the meeting is over. Details matter. Suppose you meet the potential client later. He doesn't think, "Oh, Joe probably meets with dozens of people every month, so he's probably forgotten the details of our conversation." No, he has outsized expectations of you because you are in the business. Hunters hunt, rabbits run, birds fly, and successful consultants remember conversations. Like the Geico commercial says, it's what you do.
- Team up with a noncompeting professional who already has a client relationship. Suppose an associate helps startups with IPOs. He knows nothing about controlling telecommunications costs. He mentions my services to his client and I get the sought-after phone call. The best scenario is that you don't share income with your ad-hoc partner but you do share referrals and introductions. It works out for everyone.
- Find something you can give away. It might be a terrific checklist or a special spreadsheet that performs some six-sigma calculation. Whatever it is, the act of giving is sometimes the precursor to sales. Gifts with your logo may or may not work. In contrast, knowledge and process gifts can make an impression. Early on in my practice I had dozens of golf shirts embroidered with my ICCM Consulting logo. It didn't pay off. In contrast, an article I wrote on change management for an IT Audit magazine proved to be a great way of introducing my services to new clients.
- Find a role as thought leader. Participate in professional committees, and panel discussions, and contribute to the dialogue on professional forums. Clients like to think they are bringing in top-tier talent.

Your brand

A brand is important but need not initially be expensive. Your company will not be engaged as the result of graphic arts. Some of the basics include:
- Logo
- Stationery, including envelopes
- Business card
- RGB and font file specifications, so you can exactly match color schemes for future products.
- Web/blog site

Your package should be in the form of reusable electronic templates, but if it fits your budget high-quality paper stationery and envelopes add a professional touch. In many cases you'll email a signed PDF document, so 500 sheets and 250 envelopes will usually be enough to last several years. The choice is not old school (paper) versus digital; instead, use both old and new techniques to make a statement.

Get a PO Box and use it for all correspondence. If you change offices or move your personal residence, there is no need to change any branding materials. If your budget is low, say $100-200, go to sites such as fiverr.com (or more expensive upwork.com) that provide a wide variety of bespoke graphic products. Again, you have to financially get past the first year, so use these low-cost services if you need to. Some consultants pay small fees for several versions of a given request. All these sites have newbie freelancers who will work mostly to get established, and they are often good enough. As a courtesy, tip them if you like their work.

I've mentioned it before in this book but will repeat—do not narrow your brand unless you are certain that you will never branch into other specialties. Think "transportation" rather than "cars," "chemical purity analytics" rather than "cadmium detection services." In some cases you may need to distinguish between your technical specialty and your industry experience. If you are an expert on point-of-sale systems and most of your customers are in the fast food business, what are you? A point-of-sale specialist across all industries or a more narrow point-of-sale expert for fast food businesses?

Education is the best giveaway

Clients and potential clients continually look for new information, recommendations, and perspectives. Consider casual insights and suggestions as routine giveaways. No one is likely to pay you for just an idea, but clients will pay for the *execution* of the idea if they like it. Your job is to give them plenty of ideas, in essence creating your own work. Education and ideas are your marketing workhorses. Here is how you can use free information to your advantage:

- Provide small chunks of information to the client on a routine basis, keeping your name on top of the resource pile.
- Use free information to avoid any ethical or legal boundaries. Someone in a heavily controlled government organization may not be able to accept a cheap pen with your logo on it, but she can accept as many recommendations, FYI articles, and other information as you can send.

- Take advantage of cheap (to you) industry knowledge. The only price you pay is the research and effort needed to stay on top of the game. Keep in mind that specialization is your friend; you can drill down to a level that even the experts can't reach because there are simply too many subjects and too many events happening across the world. If you're really current, you have information to give away.
- Look for spin-offs. For example, if you are giving a presentation any areas for further research you mention could become future projects.
- Send an email with one or more links to an Internet source. This saves the client the effort of doing the search. Google Docs allows an article/document to be "published" to the Web. All you need to do is send the client a link that instantly takes him to the document. Of course, avoid this technique if the material is confidential.
- Attach a copy of any recent articles you have written or a PowerPoint of a recent presentation.
- Send a copy of a book you have written so long as it is closely related to the client's needs. Do not use your book solely for a chest-thumping exercise.

Education is broader than what you find through a Google search. It includes "tribal knowledge" that comes from disparate parts of the organization, anecdotal information from past experience, and tidbits from your associates. If you have "done it" or even been in close contact with those who have, you provide a level of credibility that exceeds others (aka "armchair quarterbacks") who are merely speculating. Sales and marketing people are a particularly good source of industry knowledge. They enjoy conversation about topics they understand and typically are happy to share.

Proposals

Proposals are often the formal documentation of general agreements already reached. In other cases they are entries in a competition of consulting firms. In either case, both you and the client benefit from a written understanding of scope, price, limitations, timing, and detailed specifications. Typical contents of a proposal include:
- Proposed services
- Recommended solutions, including specific or range of costs
- Deliverables
- Timing

- Client responsibilities, e.g., ensure staff will allocate enough time to answer important questions
- Caveats (includes any major concerns; purpose is to eliminate surprises)
- Appendices
- Terms and conditions

Your response to an RFI (request for information) or an RFP (request for proposal) is a special case proposal. Besides the obvious need for clarity, proper spelling, and easily understood writing, you should pay attention to instructions. Amazingly, some vendors and consultants will ignore specific client instructions. Don't do that. Your response should be 100% compliant with both content and structure. If the client asks for your proposal in electronic form plus four copies in three-ring binders, with pricing upfront, comply without comment. If some requests are impractical or hopelessly vague, respond politely by requesting further discussion. Showing up the client's lack of knowledge has the same effect as pointing out a boss's lack of expertise in a meeting with his peers. Fatal.

As an independent consultant, one of your more important hobbies is collecting RFPs and related responses. RFPs can consume an immense amount of time. You need to have boilerplate for all of the most common requirements. For example, include the history of your company and the resources that you can bring to the project. Subcontractors and other information specific to your consulting company should be available for a cut/paste into the RFP. Spend an off day roaming the Internet and download dozens of examples. No points are awarded for originality in formatting.

Cosmetics are important for any RFI or RFP response. For the electronic version, use consistent headers, consistent fonts, and other formatting techniques. One grammatical error I see frequently is the lack of parallel construction and bullet points. For example, assume that a consultant is discussing deliverables. She might list the following:

- Review accounts payable for duplicate payments.
- Examine internal controls over new vendor setup.
- We will leave all our checklists and ratio analysis for your future system reviews.

The third bullet above is clearly not a parallel construction since the first two are action verbs with no subject and the last one is a full sentence. For consistency in formatting, use a MS Word or Google Docs style that includes appropriate, defined headers so that a table of contents can be generated automatically. Submit a PDF version of the final Word document unless the RFP specifically requests another format. If you provide your Word document there is the risk that a client could have old software or could alter formatting with an inadvertent keystroke.

If you are required to produce hard copy in addition to the electronic copy of your response the output needs to be attractive and highly organized. For example, do not use canned number tabs for notebook dividers. Instead, use a structure like "one—introduction," "two—executive summary," and so on. Don't make the client do any more flipping through your proposal than is absolutely necessary. Use tabs, headings, bullets, numbers, illustrations, and any other such techniques to speed up the experience for the individuals assessing your response. They may not even consciously realize their own bias, but I'm here to tell you that appearance and powerful organization strongly influence them. One of the ways that you win races is to bid on all the horses. Similarly, you win the RFP bid by both conscious and subconscious influences.

Researching your client's industry

Sometimes consultants maximize income by specializing in one industry or even a subspecialty within that industry. However, working in multiple industries usually provides the most consistent earnings. Varied industry experience also gives you a leg up on solutions that your client may not see. Multiple industries mean repeated research to get up to speed quickly on the dynamics of the client's business. The following are steps to speed your learning curve:

- Use Standard and Poor's industry survey for trends, competitors' strategies, and financial statements.
- Study the annual reports of several industry leaders.
- Use www.slideshare.com and similar websites to see challenges and opportunities in your client's business sector.
- Review relevant blogs and forums.
- Go to Amazon.com and use the "look inside" feature to view the table of contents in leading industry books. This will provide insight into the most important issues for that industry.
- Identify thought leaders and do a Web search for their blogs and articles.

An inconvenient problem for large firms

You can compete with large, prestigious consulting firms by stressing differences that benefit the client:

- The client is important to you. For the multimillion-dollar consulting firms, your client may be small potatoes.
- What the client gets from your firm is the best you have to offer. With larger firms there are only so many superstars available. The sales team may include a top performer, but will that person be doing the work?
- You are willing to carefully listen to not only the client's needs but also suggested approaches and philosophies. The traditional very large consulting firms are committed to their specific methodologies and sometimes ignore the client's preferences.
- You know that you either deliver or perish in the consulting business. Larger firms may have multiple groups with different agendas. For example, the sales group may go after business in which the technical delivery team only has limited expertise
- Because you are a sole proprietor or perhaps a small consulting group everyone in your firm must wear multiple hats, including client relations. A tax partner in a large consulting firm once told me that he had a tax expert on his team who he could not bring in front of the customer because of personality issues. Who knows whether the client was charged additional hours for a customer-facing intermediary.

Presenting to your client

By the time you have the opportunity to make a formal presentation you are more than halfway to the sale. At that point confirmation bias is on your side. A successful presentation combines skill, planning, and practice—lots of practice. Use the following as a starting point. The art of presentation is a book in itself:

- Keep your presentation as short as practical.
- Avoid excessive discussion regarding your consulting practice background, credentials, and other "all about me" information. We are all fascinated with ourselves; potential clients not so much.
- Finish early if possible.
- Move away from the podium.
- Don't have your PowerPoint do double duty, i.e., function as a presentation medium as well as a detailed report. Otherwise you create a slide that does neither very well.
- Use a remote-control device.
- Don't turn the lights completely off.

- Avoid engagement with disruptive participants. Nothing looks worse than a public fight. Rephrase uninformed questions so that it is clear you are taking everyone seriously. "Good question, Mr. Smith. Yes, we have considered recent reports of feral dogs entering public buildings and frightening customers. Fortunately, we have not had these problems in our urban locations."
- Keep slides to three or four bullets and reduce the number of words.
- Simplicity always works best, whether for words or for images.
- Never make a spelling or grammatical error on slides. Errors there broadcast carelessness.
- Do not blindly follow your script if it becomes obvious that part of it is not applicable or should be tabled for some other reason. For example, if you are presenting efficiency recommendations to a group of hotel managers and you discuss electric vehicle stations for the guests, you should probably skip that section if the audience is completely familiar with the topic and seems bored with what you're saying. It's a basic tenet of information theory that if your listener can predict with 100% accuracy what you're going to say next, then you are by definition not providing information. A script is not sacred. I am astounded at the number of presentations featuring, front and center, the sellers history, awards and other chest thumping artifacts. Can't they see the irritation in the eyes of the audience?
- Consider starting the presentation with a statistic or a particular insight, such as X percent of shoppers will be lost for every twenty yards they must park away from a store.
- Memorize your presentation if it is absolutely vital to your project or your position with the client. Lack of hesitation and smooth flow of words are flags that indicate to your audience that you are comfortable and knowledgeable with the material.
- Avoid generalities. Specific facts are more useful to your audience.
- Dispense with exotic or complex PowerPoint backgrounds. Do not use transitions or other attention grabbing gimmicks. You don't want your audience distracted. Also, there will typically be a certain percentage of your audience whose eyesight is suboptimal. Don't exacerbate viewing problems with small fonts or images.
- Avoid complex graphics. I've seen examples from analytics mavens with multiple layers of arrows, buttons, and comments along with a layer of abstraction that only a PhD statistician could appreciate.
- Turn off automatic updates temporarily so that you don't have an embarrassing five minutes of forced Windows update.
- Be early, always.

- Always have a backup. This means in most cases having hard-copy printouts squirreled away so that in the worst case you can hand them out. Keep in mind that you'll typically be doing presentations at the client's premises. Clients sometimes do not keep their audiovisual equipment in working order. If you feel guilty from an ecological perspective, donate to the National Forest Foundation[6].
- Always have an *electronic* backup as well. USB drives fail at inconvenient times. Carry two copies of your presentation.
- Avoid moving around too much in your slides; it can be distracting.
- Avoid jokes unless you truly are skilled at comedy. Likewise dispense with jargon—your most prized attendees are those at higher levels in the organization who may not be that familiar with your specialty.
- Schedule your presentations so that you don't interfere with events such as a product launch, crunch time (e.g., Accounting quarter end close), or just before a holiday weekend.
- Use a separate handout for details so that your presentation can be Zenlike in its simplicity and impact. I highly recommend the book *Presentation Zen* by Garr Reynolds.
- Frame your presentation as a story if appropriate. The format goes something like this: Company X had a problem. They tried to fix it by doing Y or Z. My consulting firm solved their problem by implementing A, B, and C.
- Use videos sparingly, and if used make them short. Do not video yourself. In general, do not use pictures of yourself anywhere in marketing presentations unless you are particularly attractive. I don't know why but it seems including a picture invites critical appraisal. The mere fact of inclusion implies boundless confidence in one's appearance. The client may think "he's a bit cocky, eh?"

After you get the business, you need to retain it. Following are some routine practices that will help you avoid problems:

- Begin each new project with a kickoff call or meeting.
- Send industry updates and other outside information to your client periodically.
- Have a short weekly meeting or call to go over issues and progress. Don't duck problems, and certainly eliminate as many surprises as you can.
- Create monthly or quarterly reports.

---

[6] I'm not being cynical here. The National Forest Foundation does important work in preserving pristine forests. They could use the help. See https://www.nationalforests.org/who-we-are/our-impact/category/tree-planting

- Maintain the perspective that your engagement has a finite life. This means that you will have a formal wrap-up and leave the client satisfied. It's also important that the client not feel you are simply hanging around. For some less-assertive clients, directly asking a consultant to leave is an unpleasant task. Either have specific items to be done or have a friendly, positive conversation about your last day on the project.
- Ensure that you show your value through strong data analytics as well as qualitative recommendations.
- Dress nicely, including professionally laundered shirts and blouses, etc.
- Avoid the "know it all syndrome"—it is the weak spot of many consultants who have in-depth knowledge. Showing off that knowledge in a way that diminishes the self-esteem of the client is foolish. Find a way to make it their idea or at least lead the conversation to the point that it seems an obvious conclusion. If you think you can get by in the consulting business with "works alone," then you are ignoring human dynamics; maintenance of client self-esteem is part of your job.
- Recognize your client's need to conserve time. Creating reports with excessive bulk and poor structure will alienate your client. Always provide a guidepost to the most important part and assume that (sometimes) only the executive summary will be read.

Self-imposed roadblocks

Unfortunately, it's easier than you think to set up your own, unintentional roadblocks. Here are some examples:

Overthinking the future. Some planning is necessary, but there aren't enough days in the year to anticipate every direction that your business may go. Keep an opportunistic, market-driven perspective and change course if you need to. A classic example is CRC Press (publishers). They started life as the Chemical Rubber Company, selling rubber aprons to chemical laboratories. As a marketing tool they created a small handbook that soon began to take on a life of its own. Eventually the company dropped manufacturing of rubber products and went full time into the publishing business. Lesson learned: don't plan the future so much that you can't change direction.

Artificial limits to your services/products. Suppose you are developing a technical writing business. You put together a team of experienced writers, online help system expertise, and other valuable skills. Your client asks you to take minutes in an important meeting. "We don't do minutes" is not the answer. You wouldn't be asked if it were not important. The client knows the task is below your team's skill level and appreciates your flexibility. You are a team player. You are not a snob. It will pay off.

The need for certainty. Unless you are immensely overqualified for your work, it is almost certain that you'll eventually be asked to do projects or tasks at the limits of your expertise. Relish the opportunity. You can always pay an outsider to coach you. The client doesn't care how you get to the result.

EXPERTISE

Brag once, succeed many times

CHOOSING THE RIGHT MOMENT in the sales cycle to show your skills is an acquired art. At the point of a possible sale you need to talk about your expertise, your ability to learn quickly, and the hardscrabble life you had while earning your spurs. The client is looking at your confidence and ability to project skill in subject matter, human relationships, and self-control. After your "elevator speech," turn the conversation away from yourself and toward solving the client's problems. After your clients (or potential clients) hear your expertise story and buy into it, they are looking only to results going forward. To repeatedly say you are top dog, especially before results are in, suggests fear and lack of confidence. Who is being convinced?

In the 1990s PipelineX[7], like many other large firms at the time, was transitioning away from mainframe computers to a client/server/open network technical architecture. Many new technologies were under review. One of PipelineX's IT providers, let's call them XYZ, stood proudly at the table with the words "I can do that" taped to their account manager's forehead. Beyond that, every major presentation, even five years into the relationship, started out with a briefing on XYZ's overarching expertise in every subject, from "TCP/IP" to distilling moonshine. Nothing was beyond their ken, at least in their own mind. The reality was a mix of success and failure. Failure in new technology is relatively common; failure with arrogance and disrespect not so much.

---

[7] A company that came to an ignoble end at a later date. I'd prefer to leave it as an unknown, although some Houston natives will undoubtedly recognize the company.

Expected skill sets

Whether your practice is in engineering, marketing, or remediation of radioactive waste, certain skills are expected. Make sure you have these core competencies:

- Project management skills. In practice this may be nothing more than Microsoft Project competency. Know more than simply using Project as a typewriter—understand scheduling, resource management, varying work weeks (e.g., six-day work weeks), percentage of completion, and other methodologies.
- Desktop competence. Calendaring, outlining, PowerPoints, spreadsheets (including pivot tables), flowcharts, and all sorts of canned visuals (e.g., red—yellow-green stoplight graphic as a status indicator) are expected. This is an area where you need to be better than your client.
- Efficiency in running meetings. Don't go into an important meeting without an agenda. Do minutes. Provide status updates in the meeting.
- Report writing. Templates and standard/boilerplate text are immensely helpful in creating professional-looking reports.
- Conference calling and Web sessions. If you have these basic communication tools well rehearsed, you may be the only person in the room who can mechanically make things happen. Technology changes daily. Keep current.

The myth of doing what you love

How many people earn a living doing what they would do anyway? One person aspires to be musical, another to marketing financial investments to the wealthy, and a third to inventing the ultimate solvent to clean up industrial waste. Problem: nearly all people on this planet make a living by doing what they are good at, not what they love. In some cases there is overlap, but usually not that much.

Why is this relevant to consulting? Because to make a living you'll need to take on nearly any project that comes your way, at least at first. So, consider the boring projects—those that are repetitive and don't build skills—as a cost of doing business. From my own experience doing Sarbanes-Oxley compliance work, I can vouch for the tedium of the work after the first few iterations, but every SOX project put me in front of more clients and eventually I was able to branch out. Don't let boring projects discourage you.

Gaining expertise

Your primary source of expertise is always direct experience. Having many projects and many clients builds your skill set like nothing else. Of course, you'll need to prepare (on your own time) for any new project before going after the business. That means intense study, with every tool available. Research has shown that the best way to learn detailed material is to read it on paper. Annotation in the margins, highlighting key passages, and outlining all contribute to cementing facts to memory. Recent polls of college students, presumably the most tech savvy demographic in the world, show a strong preference for paper textbooks over their electronic counterpart.[8] One specific method mentioned by memory experts is the "method of loci", which is based on the ancient technique of attaching facts to physical places.

And lest you think I'm a technophobe—there's an Amazon Kindle in my briefcase, another one on my nightstand, and another one in my study. However, I recognize that words on physical paper are the surest route to facts and concepts that need to be retained. The past and future are not mutually exclusive. MS Office 2016, Google Docs, and a #2 lead pencil coexist nicely.

Beyond purposeful reading, the physical act of writing important concepts provides a special boost to learning not available from just reading. A million years of human evolution have created a synergy between abstract concepts and the hand movements we call writing. Take advantage of it.

There are many ways to gain expertise, beyond using our most excellent friend Mr. Google. Examples include:

- Handwrite a mind map showing relationships between concepts, action items, people, places, and facts. Include most anything connected to a project or consulting assignment. If you prefer a more-formal mind map presentation, use software such as iMindmap (www.imindmap.com), Mindjet, Xmind, Coggle, Freemind or Mindnode.
- Write an article about a topic and get it published. Nothing concentrates the mind more than writing about a topic that is new to you. Publishers of newsletters, blogs, and magazines are constantly looking for new material, so your chances of being published are high. Go through a checklist of good writing techniques and have someone else read the manuscript before submission. Some writers read their drafts out loud to identify possible errors.
- Use YouTube. It is not just for learning how to paint.

---

[8] Michael S. Rosenwald, "Why Digital Natives Prefer Reading Print," *Washington Post* (February 22, 2015).

- Call people in your relevant professional organization. It is OK to ask favors if you are willing to do the same for others. Five minutes on the phone with someone who has been there is a good use of your time.
- Use free, online courses from major universities (sometimes called MOOCs, "massive open online courses"). Harvard, MIT, and other top-tier universities often make some of their courses available to the public.

In gaining deep expertise, another friend is Google Scholar. When you use Google Scholar you're automatically dispensing with most of the hype, advertisements, sales, and other distortions of the facts. You can typically find professional research articles that cover any topic in great depth and with a reasonably balanced perspective. In fact, if you are asked to opine on some subject by your clients, you would do well to make use of this specialized search engine. It typically provides the most up-to-date and detailed information available.

Specialization

The great thing about specialization is that it never ends. For example, years ago attorneys specializing in information technology or telecom contracts were rare. Now there are attorneys who have made a name for themselves in niches as small as Oracle license contract negotiation. The key is to have multiple specialties so that your work is diversified enough to withstand constant industry changes. Some specializations don't even have a name. For example, you can specialize in being an "intelligent person with both excellent overall skills and desktop proficiency." No one would ever say that, but that's what they want. Here is one scenario: discuss issues with all tiers of management, assemble a set of detailed Visio process flowcharts, develop a dynamic PowerPoint presentation with some tasteful animation, lead team meetings, send out MS Project Gantt charts, and write a report with recommendations, to be stored on the client's content management system. Perhaps there is no single step in a complex engagement that is particularly difficult. What you bring to the table is a single, trustworthy resource for completing all the project management tasks. From your client's perspective, it would be inconvenient to acquire various resources from an outside firm to do individual parts of the project. Contrary to popular opinion, being a "jack of all trades" is valuable since it reduces administrative friction. Consider the steps required for your client to bring someone in—they have to create a contract (SOW) for the work, a master agreement, and a nondisclosure document. In some cases the documents need to be reviewed by multiple parties. Better to go through this process once with you rather than multiple times with a group of specialists.

Like moths that evolve to fit new habitats, consulting work constantly morphs to satisfy changing client needs. It never stops. The key is to have multiple specialties so that your work is diversified enough to withstand perpetual industry changes.

Buzzwords don't get any respect

As consultants we sometimes hear jokes at our own expense. They are typically good natured, such as: "Know what is black and brown and looks good on a consultant? Answer: a Doberman pinscher. How many consultants does it take to change a lightbulb? Answer: How much money do you have?" Some of this ribbing comes from the use of TLAs (three-letter acronyms), buzzwords, and the MBA/Harvard/Stanford fad of the day. Nonetheless, it's your bread and butter. You have to know enough canned techniques to deliver value on the spot. Stock terms like "gap analysis" should be your second language. You simply do not have the time to create consultant processes from scratch every time.

The following is a sampling of stock processes/concepts that you should know. Since the items do not necessarily fit into any one category, I'll borrow a term from IT—"blob" (technically a binary large object). Blobs are like science fiction shape formers and can be anything. And yes, many of them are trite, clichéd, and boring. Think of a dentist working on an elderly patient. He sees work that may have been discontinued fifty years ago but he still needs to understand what was done. You need to know some of the old techniques along with the new ones because it marks you as well educated. That being said, you certainly don't need to implement an older, hashed over business technique. Clients sometimes use them; following is a partial list:

- SWOT—Strengths, weaknesses, opportunities, and threats. Usually shown as a square split into quarters.
- Paradigm shift.
- ROI—Return on investment.
- MBWA—Management by walking around. How executives can avoid dangerous isolation.
- LCP—Low-cost producer.
- SOX—Sarbanes-Oxley act. Many firms have control systems in place solely to comply with this legislation. Enron was one of the high-profile failures that inspired the legislation.
- M&A—Mergers and acquisitions.
- TQM—Total quality management.

- Think outside the box.
- Be creative and look for novel solutions.
- Value-chain analysis.
- An analysis tool to identify your client's core competencies and how cost advantage and differentiation can be optimized at each stage of the value chain.
- Five forces, from Michael Porter's work at Harvard: threat of new entrants; threat of substitute products or services; bargaining power of customers (buyers); bargaining power of suppliers; intensity of competitive rivalry.
- Scalable—Across-the-board concept stating that certain processes may or may not be able to double, triple, or increase by any multiple. For example, the owner of a small business controls his business by counting cash at the end of each day. That works with 50-100 customers per day but not with 5,000 customers. The process of counting cash by the owner does not scale.
- First-mover advantage—The competitive advantage that a company earns by being the first to enter a specific market or industry. Sometimes the advantage goes to the second entrant. For example, in the early days of aviation, Curtis's airplane designers enabled the company to dominate the market because they could see the shortcomings of the Wright brother's models.
- Gap analysis—Comparison of actual performance of an entity or process with the desired performance.
- Actionable—Recommendations should be structured so that something specific can be done rather than offer a "do better" platitude.

Strengths	Weaknesses	
High bargaining power suppliers Good reputation Diversified portfolio Big influence on the market Good R&D department Economies of scale Big capital reserves	Structural inertia High transaction costs Weak focus on process innovations No focus on private sector	Internal
Emerging new markets Technological developments Technological lock-in of products Demand for saver equipment	Low bargaining power buyers Highly regulated industry Products copied easily Ethical pressure Economic crisis Prices of raw material fluctuate highly	External
Opportunities	Threats	

Example of SWOT Analysis

Becoming a subject-matter expert

Selling business and subject-matter expertise are inextricably connected. Getting to that state—knowing a lot relative to your peers—requires that you travel down multiple paths. First, mingle with people who know. Formal training, books, and other media will rarely include all the subtleties of your practice area. Talking with experts gives you a sense of what is important, the typical choke points and expanded sources of expertise. Rubbing elbows with experts does not necessarily have to be physical meetings. Email exchanges and online forums work too, especially if you observe the forum guidelines.

Next, acquire credentials. If your credential, such as a CPA or PE (professional engineer), is viewed as difficult to obtain, it will outweigh several lightweight certifications. Having the right three- or four-letter designation behind your name is the ultimate elevator speech. I earned a CPA certificate early in my career even though I knew accounting was not my direction. The certification itself helped me land business and charge higher rates. If you have no certification now and cannot devote the time to acquiring one with high industry recognition, at least get a minor certificate so that you can put some initials behind your name on your business card. At the same time, avoid certifications so unrecognizable that they appear contrived.

Awards and formal recognition will certainly burnish your reputation for expertise. Meaningful recognition from high-profile organizations suggests both skill and ambition. Make every effort to list something like "outstanding contributor to the profession, from the Institute of X" on your resume. From the client's perspective, there are many people who can take an assignment and complete it. There aren't that many who will go beyond formal instructions and creatively add value. As is true of business in general, the distribution of consulting fees is lopsided in favor of those who distinguish themselves; "winner take all" is built into the business culture, particularly in the United States.

Your influence in industry and your area of specialization also strongly affects your success. For example, if you participate in the appropriate forums and professional groups, you might be asked by a senior manager in the Department of Commerce to comment on proposed regulation. Drop that into casual conversation with a potential client; it could seal the deal.

If you are in a place in life where major educational or professional certifications are not feasible, do not despair. It may be a bit more work, but success is certainly achievable. Clients are looking for expertise, experience, communications skills and emotional IQ more than layers of formal educational varnish.

Self-doubt

Uncertainty is built into the human condition. Consulting is a business where you are presenting yourself as an expert with full knowledge that you are not expert in everything. In the first few weeks or months you may have bad dreams about the client asking you something where you not only failed to know the specific answer but you don't even know the general topic. With the rate of change in business, society, and technology today, it's going to happen. In the world of IT for example there is probably a new programming language created every day. The number of cell phone applications is estimated at well over one million. It helps to recognize on the front that you will miss some areas. The solution is to find out the answer soon as you can, read every day, and always let the client know of your relative certainty on any particular answer. It's one thing to not know something, it's another thing to present that you know and get the wrong answer. So when you're nagged by self-doubt keep in mind that no one truly expects expertise on everything all the time. What they do expect is sincerity, eagerness to find the answer, willingness to share those answers and help in resolving problems. I saw a cartoon once that showed a consultant with his arms folded telling the client that the problem was really bad and that someone needed to fix it. He was blithely unaware that he was the dude that should fix it.

Clients evaluate you far more on your attentiveness and eagerness to deliver the results. Did you listen to what they actually said? If they ask you to be there at 8 o'clock were you? Did you research any topics that came up in discussions that you did not understand? Did you ask the client to clarify some items that were either ambiguous or specific to her company so that an outsider would need additional explanation. And finally the best way to ultimately support self-doubt is simply to take action. Do things, evaluate the results and improve your process. Action begets skill. The more action, the more skill.

Do you deserve success?

This is not a silly question. People are sometimes unaware of subconscious messages they have received over the years, starting from childhood. As an example, consider that many winners of the lottery lose all their money within a year or two. Why? They would probably give you all sorts of answers, perhaps greedy relatives or bad investments or a gambling addiction. The real reason is most likely that their new wealth created a major cognitive dissonance in their life. All their friends and associates typically live in a narrow socioeconomic zone. Perhaps they've never been in a restaurant with cloth napkins (I've been in places in south Texas where this is typical). Maybe their new mansion is in a neighborhood with highly educated professionals and executives who have little in common with a *nouveau riche* lottery winner. So, their subconscious mind nudges them towards choices that will restore their former emotional support system. Their hidden brain commands: "Get rid of the money." For all of us there are hidden forces that influence our choices. To be successful, you must not only envision success – financial, personal fulfillment, and new opportunities – but also believe that it is okay to do so. Success means that you'll be sometimes out of your comfort zone, both socially and from a business perspective. It's okay.

General skills

Skills in communications, discovery, presentation, and team leadership are expected, regardless of your specialty. Inventory your skills and fill in the gaps. The following is a list of generic capabilities most clients expect on day one of the assignment:

- Basic analytics: Unless you are specifically in the business of big data/analytics, you will not need to be a statistician. However, you can add a lot to any project by using simple analytical tools (available in Excel, Tableau, and other packages). One caveat – even if a statistic, such as number of standard deviations from the mean, is easily calculated, do not use it unless you understand the concept.
- Basic charts: Illustrate trends (right click on graph points to insert a trend line), distribution of dollars, such as percentage of customers versus their contribution to revenue, outliers, ratios, and many others. For example, a dishonest employee of one of my clients had been siphoning off cash by altering product return records. A quick line chart of the ratio of returns to sales for all stores combined versus the one being reviewed showed a spike that persisted as long as the employee continued the theft. Presented visually, the fraud was obvious. The charts need not be sophisticated. For example, charts published in the Wall Street Journal are typically simple, with a minimum of chart clutter.
- Statistical samples: Sometimes gathering information is too time consuming to answer management-level questions such as "Are our approval procedures for capital expenditures working as specified by policy?" Tracking down details and step-by-step actions is not practical for thousands or hundreds of thousands of transactions. However, a statistically valid sampling often serves to answer the questions. There are many types of sampling techniques such as dollar unit sampling, but you can often get what you need by simply adding a column in Excel next to the date data of interest, then inserting random numbers using the =rand() function, sorting on the random number, and selecting the top 10 or 100 rows. It's a quick and simple approach.
- Outliers/exception techniques: Use some of Excel's many tools to identify anomalies and data. There are thousands of possible exceptions.

Some example techniques used to identify outliers and exceptions include:
- Duplicates. Two paid invoices with same vendor number and invoice number.
- Use Excel functions to find largest, smallest, negative, or positive numbers where there should be none. Check for ratios that don't make sense;

transactions that are unexpectedly old or new, current inventory showing an odd value, etc.

- Identifying (key) numbers or codes with no match, such as invoices with customer numbers having no match on the organization's CRM or customer tables.
- Unexpected gaps in records, e.g., days with no or abnormally few transactions, or skipped numbers where each entry should be one more than the previous entry.
- Odd trends—sudden jumps up or down in quantities or dollars over time.
- Unexpected aging results, e.g., a high number of past-due customers.
- Review of time series data in a low level of detail or a summary level, but different from the client's normal view. For example, the client may always get reports based on fiscal month but some interesting trends might become apparent by looking at the same data on a weekly basis.

Organizations today expect competence with numeric analysis and even big data reporting. You should thoroughly understand the basics of Excel (allocate learning time, not just on-the-job training). If you receive a spreadsheet and have five minutes to comment on the data, it should be second nature to highlight the numbers, press F11, and see the chart. It might not be exactly what you need, but you've taken advantage of your mind's amazingly quick pattern-recognition ability.

Skill self-assessment

Know the limits of your skills and the suitability of your toolset. Clients are reluctant to spend time with you to describe in excessive detail what they need; they want to generalize and for you to fill in the gaps. You could start the project using Excel and then later recognize that Excel is not suitable for the scale and size of the request—the IT group should use an ERP development tool such as Oracle or SAP tools to develop the system. Users can inadvertently shoot themselves (and you) in the foot by not providing specifications up front. Don't fall into the snake pit.

The highest-paid independent consultants are those with deep interpersonal skills and an ability to quickly simulate sufficient qualitative and quantitative information to present at least preliminary findings to management. For example, let's assume you are brought in to review IT expenses and assess potential areas of savings and their dollar impact. What to do? The following is a typical process:

1. Prepare your analysis plan—what data is needed and what will your deliverables be?

2. Request general ledger data (including account structure) and payables data for the company.

3. Identify capital and expense categories specifically charged to the IT department. You could also look for related changes not coded to the IT group.

4. Use payables and accounting data at the lowest available level of detail. Begin summarizing the data based on a variety of criteria. If the data is voluminous, use expanded tools such as Excel power pivot or R.

5. Ask relevant data model questions:

   - How much do I spend on mobile computing? Per employee? What are the outliers and why? Is the client spending excessive dollars on the latest gadgets?
   - What are the costs of telecom infrastructure, personnel, and other categories?
   - Could the client outsource part of the function and save money?
   - Have any costs gone up dramatically over a three-year period?
   - Are there abrupt changes, such as a large increase in communication line charges, that suggest the client may have gone past a contract end date? For example, most telecommunications carriers will charge the client the contract rate until it expires and after that charge a significantly higher monthly fee until a new contract is negotiated.
   - How does the client's summarized expenses compare to others in their industry? (Access Gardner.com or similar services to provide comparison data).
   - Has a thorough review of costs been conducted lately? If not, you can assume an industry rule of thumb of about 5 to 10% possible reductions as a result of a detailed analysis.

Typically, an engagement will either be an overview, highlighting areas of potential success, or a drill-down project to achieve those potential savings. If you are brought in to deliver savings and document the hard numbers, be sure to budget the considerable time required to collect invoices, show before-and-after numbers, and prepare detailed schedules.

One of your "hobbies" should be the study of communicating complex/detailed information simply and intuitively. Early in my career a Vice President of Internal Audit asked me to create a model of a computer system he wanted to discuss with the board of directors. I was astonished by what he really wanted — a shoebox with simple pictures, colored pipe cleaner wires and a few other kindergarten type items. He took the "model," used it in his presentation and came back from the director's meeting pleased with the results. I'm betting there were some snickers at the meeting but in the end, it worked. The toy model was clear, direct and concrete. After hearing so many other presentations, with layer upon layer of abstraction, they liked the simplicity. Never say things like "... we noted that zinc ores delivered to the processing station approximately conform to a Poisson arrival distribution and therefore ...." Unless you know, for sure, that your executive audience understands the nuts and bolts of the business, stay away from presenting details at that level. It does not impress. It alienates.

Bill Yarberry, CPA

BUILD POWERFUL CLIENT RELATIONSHIPS

The "good-person" image

BEFORE ANYTHING ELSE, you must project yourself as trustworthy. Put yourself in the shoes of the client. Picking the wrong consultant is costly in dollars, time, and organizational reputation. What criteria is used to select the winner from competing consulting firms?

- Formal criteria: professional qualifications, education, peer recommendations, experience in the field.
- Appearance: appropriate professional dress, absence of obvious signs of sloppiness, and nothing that deviates from what other professionals wear. You are there to sell business, not to tout your sartorial mastery. Unless you are in the rarest of circles, your bulgari magsonic sonnerie tourbillon watch will not be noticed.
- Unconscious influences: overall projection of stability and reliability. You must appear to be a person whose personal life has *constraints*. Family, hobbies, sports, and participation in social/charitable organizations are all activities that constrain you to a predictable and therefore reliable way of life. As a buyer, the potential client will usually choose the most qualified but also the most trustworthy consultant. Clients do not need to know what happened to you at parties that may have gotten out of hand. No drunk stories, ever. No one will tell you this. Indeed, most buyers are completely unaware of their unconscious selection process.

Responsiveness, the secret sauce

How quickly do you respond to your client's email or text? It doesn't matter that you are working furiously on her project; responsiveness tells the client how important she is to you. Answer soon. It matters.

In some cases, it is not possible to actually do anything, but you can still let the client know you'll get back with her shortly. It's the long silence that sours the relationship. Obviously, you can't drop everything at a moment's notice but you can respond. Showing irritation under stress is a luxury you cannot afford. Think the client has never experienced stress?

Ego feeding

We all need praise and self-esteem. Napoleon remarked, "I have discovered men will risk their lives, even die, for ribbons!" Strutting in front of the client is a thoroughly human temptation, but you are there to succeed in business, not boost your own self-esteem. So, at every moment, consider how things look through the lens of the client. It may seem unfair—sometimes the client talks about his problems or accomplishments and never acknowledges your needs, but so what? Listen. The more you listen the better the client feels. Believe me, listening is the sweet spot for the consultant. The client may have a toxic boss and hypercompetitive peers. You may be the first person all day who has actually listened with empathy. Listening pays.

The right kind of gifts

In the Viking days leaders like Ragnar Lothbrok and Harald Blatand gained followers both by winning victories and by distributing gifts. Gifts, such as precious metal rings, were an expected marker of leadership. The same principle, minus the actual warfare, applies today. Maintaining an image of largess and unselfishness suggests you care and have energy to spare. In contrast, greed and calculations of profit to the tenth decimal place suggest insecurity and a propensity for unfairness. Important people, successful people, don't go fishing and count worms at the bait store.

A small effort (giving away some time) goes a long way toward your image as a good person. Should you take the time to hold the door open for the maintenance guy? Someone will notice. Write an Excel macro that saves an AP clerk from some drudgery? That gets noticed, too. If the effort becomes routine or takes more than a few minutes of your time, then a discussion about billable hours becomes reasonable and expected.

Consultant's etiquette

Good manners are required everywhere; there are a few additional ones for the consultant. Avoid breaking the illusion that your current client—when you are on premises—is more important than any other business you have going on at the moment. Take a call from client A when you are working for client B, but step outside if the call takes more than a few minutes. And of course, be sure to deduct the time off client B's invoice. Don't double dip on billable hours, even for ten minutes.

Small gestures count. While doing some audit work for a media company in Florida, I learned the value of client empathy. The CIO had been told he would be fired if his firm did not pass tests of compliance with Sarbanes-Oxley legislation. I was one of a half dozen consultants putting in some long hours to get to the deadline. One Saturday we were at the office with the CIO and everyone but me decided to take a long lunch hour at an upscale restaurant in Boca Raton. Rather than leave the CIO by himself, I decided to stay and have a Subway sandwich at my desk. The empathy paid off; I was put in charge of the work team and was able to bill additional hours to wrap up the project. Lesson learned: don't party when the big cheese is stressed out.

Don't be a skinflint at the office. When someone at the client's office is having a baby shower, don't give the admin $5 and ask for some change back. Like Caesar's wife, a successful consultant is beyond reproach. Consider generosity for social events at the office as a business expense. When you bring in kolaches on Friday morning, bring the best. It helps to have everyone in your court. Be especially nice to the admin. Don't even think of giving the executive a holiday basket without giving one to her assistant. The executive approving your invoice may not say it, but she's highly sensitive to how you are viewed by her staff.

What not to do: two examples

Sometimes we get a bad idea and then act it out before thinking it through. Following are two client relations mistakes, one made by a subcontractor I once used and the other by me. This kind of learning is like sticking your finger in a light socket. It's painful, but it certainly ingrains the lessons in memory:

Lesson #1: Subcontractor jumps the rails of appropriate behavior. I brought in a subcontractor to do some security analysis for a client. The subcontractor, let's call him "Al", was competent and eager for the work. Unfortunately, he broke two unwritten rules. First, he roamed through my client's offices attempting to find executives willing to listen to his own sales pitch. A sub should never co-opt the business of the consultant who brings him in. Secondly and more seriously, he decided on the spur of the moment to run a live security test that we had not discussed with the client. This engagement was supposed to be a standard compliance review, with no surprises expected. Highly irritated, the client called us both into his office to "clarify" how the engagement was supposed to work. I never used Al again, for anything. Lesson learned for me: always go over the unwritten rules and political realities with any subs before they step into the client's premises.

Lesson #2: Jumping into vanity. I walked into a client's office and noticed a well-known text book that I had contributed to. Without thinking it through, I pulled the book off the shelf and showed her my chapter. She graciously acknowledged my contribution to the profession. Maybe she was privately annoyed at my thinly disguised boasting. I'll never know. One thing is for sure — such displays of chest thumping contribute nothing to consulting success and may rankle the client. I was not there to service my personal need for approbation. I was there to provide whatever professional services were required by the client. Lesson to self: *think* why you are there!

The upside of office politics

What do Santa Claus, the Easter Bunny, and the upside of office politics have in common? None of them are real. Make every effort to stay away from the emotional undercurrent. Inappropriate behaviors by employees often lurk just under the surface. Ignore them. You are not "Dear Abbey." Avoid emotional entanglement and judging client personnel. No value added there.

Perhaps most important to your consulting business is the recognition that your hidden agenda is to make clients feel good about themselves. That includes rookie staff as well as senior executives. Organizations are remarkably reluctant to openly praise employees. Your offhand comment will be noticed; you may be the only person who has actually said anything positive *out loud*. Subtle and truthful praise is powerful.

Winners and losers

Common sense tells us to treat the person who authorizes our invoice payment with consideration. Beyond that obvious practice, you need to broaden your social strategy. Effective relationship building includes a plethora of direct and indirect actions you can take to extend your long-term business.

Competition drives organizational life. This means that winners and losers will constantly be created. The losers will get their pay/power reduced, and in many cases, lose their jobs. The relevance to you is that in most cases the losers find new jobs in new firms. A "loser" is only a loser at one point in time, in one situation and at one particular company. In their new position, they might remember you from the old job. They might bring you in.

A mid-tier technical manager at one of my clients was fired, primarily because his organizational skills were not at the level demanded by the new CIO. He was an interesting fellow with plenty of stories to tell; we had occasional conversations during my project. When he was terminated I expressed sympathy and wished him well. Two years later came an unexpected call. He had recommended me to one of his peers at an oil and gas services firm. The job was over 500 hours and indirectly led to another lucrative job in the same industry.

The takeaway is this: people hurt when they lose political fights or get fired. They get talked about, suffer loss of self-esteem, and will likely be depressed. You are independent and above the fray. Help them in any way you can, including contacts, recommendations, and most importantly a show of confidence in their abilities. Failing in a specific job is not the same as failure in general. You were never part of their organization and you may be able to provide some balanced perspective when it is needed the most. Peter Drucker, one of the most respected management advisors of the last fifty years, asked, "Why should people who, for 10 or 15 years, have been competent suddenly become incompetent? The reason in practically all cases I have seen, is that people continue in their new assignment to do what made them successful in the old assignment and what earned them the promotion. Then they turn incompetent, not because they have become incompetent, but because they are doing the wrong things."

Stay out of dogfights

If you have a particularly good relationship with a client manager or executive, it is tempting to get involved in the business soap opera of the day. Don't. There is no upside for you. Treat all the same so that you don't have to pick winners to get future business.

There is an unspoken expectation that you will remain apart from your client's social struggles. If Mr. X comes in looking haggard and is unproductive until the late AM, best to appear unaware of the slack performance. It is not your job to make the world safe from Mr. X.

Small gestures matter

Suppose you are at a client where several other consultants/vendors are providing services in the same department. You are the only consultant to bring in kolaches and breakfast tacos. Most will not give it a thought, but some will recognize your effort to stand in line to buy fifty snacks and lug them back to the office. It is a tiny step to your "good-person" image.

There are countless other micro favors you can do: donate blood at the client office, help the exec admin move tables for a staff event, spend a few minutes writing an Excel macro to save someone time—whatever can be done to show that you appreciate all client personnel (not simply those with power to affect billable hours or project fees). All of us make mistakes. Your chances of forgiveness go up dramatically if you are seen as a person who cares for the group.

Sincerity is as important as generosity. It's hard to fake. One of my first supervisors at PricewaterhouseCoopers in Memphis had a penchant for building up and then inadvertently tearing down relationships. An engineering graduate of MIT and a dedicated professional, he made every effort to "mind meld" with his clients in order to learn useful information that could help sales. We were riding to lunch one day with a couple of clients when one of them provided a valuable, highly relevant nugget of information. Without thinking, my supervisor said, "Great. Now that I know that, no need to take you guys to lunch." It was said as a joke, but somehow it was not a joke—and it was not perceived as a joke. Sincerity counts.

EXECUTION

Architect your consulting process

THERE IS A PLETHORA of selling and implementation processes. You should pick one or more of them, modify to suit, and then tweak for the rest of your career. The following are some example steps to be included in your consultancy process:

- Identify the client's goal. What problem(s) need to be solved?
- Develop a solution or at least a going-in approach to finding a solution or answer.
- Quantify your potential solution. If your client engages you to do X, then he can expect a savings of Y or a payback within Z months.
- Plan the work, including plenty of detail (dates, milestones, decision points, status reporting, etc.).
- If you bring in subcontractors make sure it is clear that you accept full responsibility for their work.
- Submit a proposal. Do not try to trick the client by burying your fees in small print at the back of the proposal. Most people look for the cost first. Do not frustrate this natural inclination. Just make the rest of the proposal attractive, well organized, and easy to read.
- Report the results at both the executive and detail levels.
- Transfer spreadsheets, documents, or multimedia that the client has paid for. Usually your work product, paid for by the client, is considered "work for hire." All related intellectual property (IP) accrues to them. And even if it is not something the client has paid for, be generous with ideas. There really isn't much new under the sun, so don't sweat IP unless it is truly unique to

you. Lots of people have high-level ideas while taking a shower or jogging; implementation of those concepts is far more challenging.

Incidentally—speaking of IP— getting a patent is a long process but certainly doable. Consider the following illustration attached to patent application number U.S. 12/138,918. The title of the patent application is "Optimized Communication Billing Management System."[9] Apparently the applicants could not be bothered to use a flowchart package for their illustrations and simply drew it on a napkin. Looking at the summary description, it certainly does not look revolutionary or completely novel to me. The point is, not every patent involves rocket science. A patent would look nice on your bio.

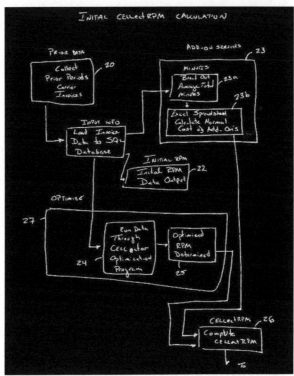

Example Diagram from Patent Application

---

[9] https://www.google.com/patents/US20080319879, Optimized Communication Billing Management System U.S. 20080319879 A1, accessed July 23, 2017.

MAXIMIZE YOUR INCOME

Bypass the middleman

A S AN INDEPENDENT CONSULTANT one of your greatest strengths is your ability to undercut larger firms on price while maintaining your quality level and earning a good rate. In some cases you may want to accept work through another consulting firm, but it should always be your second choice. The disadvantages of working through someone else include:

- Giving up at least one-third of your rate. Many "body shops" charge the client twice the rate that the person doing the work receives.
- Your creativity can be stifled. Working through a firm to serve the end client means that you have to work following the guidelines of both the client and the intermediary firm.
- You are typically prohibited from approaching the client for a year or two, based on standard consulting agreements.
- Working for two bosses (the intermediate firm and the end client) can be stressful. Double the politics, double the personal agendas.
- Once you are a proven resource, clients would prefer to bring you in directly, if they can. Your independent rates are typically below what they can get when going through a larger firm.

Your unique brain

Let's suppose you are comparing yourself to Sally. She's a great speaker, people smart, plays good politics, and can tear apart a complex financial instrument. There's a voice in your head that says, "Compared to her, I lose." You think she'll get the project every time. But wait, there's a little more to the story. The beauty of twenty-first century professional life is that specialties endlessly divide and multiply, seemingly faster than people can catch up. You win by specializing. So please, ignore general comparisons and focus on the specifics that make money for you. Recognize that your brain is unique. Similarly, your consulting practice has a "USP" – unique selling point. Or it may have two or three. Your USP is a proven method for showing your capabilities to best advantage.

Increasing your fees

Both new and old consultants wrestle with fee structures. Some consulting books will tell you authoritatively that you can double your fees simply by stressing to the client how important your work is. And indeed, that may work in some situations. My take is that when starting out, you should price your services between what "body shops" pay their employees and what the client would typically pay the body shop. For example, ABC services company may provide consultants at $175 per hour but pay their employees $90 per hour. In that environment, a good starting place would be around $130 per hour for your fee. As you grow in experience and reputation, you can adjust your rates based on your client relationship, city, and industry. If your consulting business is mainly over the Internet, your pricing will most likely be influenced by reputation rather than your geographic location.

One advantage of repeat business is the ability to gently increase your fees over time. It is not difficult for the person or department that brings you in to justify an increase of five or $10 each year. An important part of pricing is to not evoke a sense of greediness or making a fast buck. If you put your immediate client's contact in a position of justifying your increase without anything concrete to point to, then the client may balk at supporting the increase. Never bump your rate on your invoice without a clear discussion with the client. If you later say "well, it was just a year-end adjustment for inflation" it still sounds faintly dishonest. Years ago, there was a television commercial for Holiday Inn which magnified the unpleasant side of surprises. That applies equally well to business. Both good and negative surprises are undesirable from the consultant's point of view. Many people at the management level regard surprises as an indication that their organization is out of control. You don't want to be in the firing line when this happens.

You may be in a position where it is easier to simply work more billable hours rather than raise your rates. I was talking with a fellow consultant at lunch one day and mentioned I needed to raise my rates with a client. I had not increased rates for this client in three years. My friend said, "no problem, just work more hours." My response was that I was already working a long workweek and more hours could affect the quality of my work, not to mention the negative effect on home life. Try always to set your rates based on where you want to be financially, within the constraints of the market. Occasionally, there are exceptions. For example, if you are charging a flat fee for a project, you could inadvertently underestimate the effort required. Aside from such billing vagaries, avoid excessive hours. Working to exhaustion will not get you to $250K annual income.

Scope creep

It's human nature to add "just one more thing." In a fixed cost engagement, you have to be concerned when clients ask for more coverage, data, research or analytics. Small items are okay but you need to be careful about setting precedent. Otherwise the expectations will be that a significant amount of free work can be tacked on to the end of any paid project. You can address this "freebie cascade" by telling the client that it appears the project needs additional work. Then send her a short proposal for the additional work. It also helps to define the work in detail upfront so that the scope itself is clear. "Just look around and tell me what needs fixing" is not sufficient direction to start a project. Develop your boilerplate and define the obvious: When will you start work? What facilities will you need from the client? Will this be purely consulting/recommendations or is implementation assistance required? Does this include international locations? Does the project require training client staff in some technology or procedure? If any code is written, is it considered "work for hire?" The more questions upfront, the less chance of later disputes.

Bill Yarberry, CPA

ICEBERGS

Employee versus independent contractor

THE IRS DOES NOT APPRECIATE employers who classify workers as contract when in fact they are functioning as employees. At the same time human resources and the legal department of many firms are looking to ensure that no independent contractors are working under conditions that would suggest they are employees. Companies have been successfully sued by independent workers who claim that they were employees in all but name. The workers claimed lost benefits such as vacation and sick time.

This may not seem like much of an issue to you, but it could be. First, you want to avoid anything that is a potential liability or embarrassment to the client. Second, you may meet all the characteristics of an independent contractor (see below) but your subcontractors might be a problem. Example: A human resources manager for one of my clients called me into her office to discuss the status of one of my subcontractors. This sub was a recent college graduate, had no other clients of her own, and failed the test of independence in other ways as well. To protect my relationship with the client, I agreed to have the sub become a temporary employee of the client to avoid even the appearance of skirting around the regulations. I lost the income from using the sub but avoided a potentially serious risk for the client.

There is no single factor that separates independent contractor from an employee, but the IRS website provides some general guidelines. Facts that provide evidence of the degree of control and independence fall into three categories:

- Behavioral: Does the company control or have the right to control what the worker does and how the worker does his or her job?

- Financial: Are the business aspects of the worker's job controlled by the payer? These include things like how the worker is paid, whether expenses are reimbursed, who provides tools/supplies, etc.
- Type of Relationship: Are there written contracts or employee type benefits (i.e., pension plan, insurance, vacation pay, etc.)? Will the relationship continue and is the work performed a key aspect of the business?
- Overall assessment: Businesses must weigh all these factors when determining whether a worker is an employee or independent contractor. Some factors may indicate that the worker is an employee, while other factors indicate that the worker is an independent contractor. There is no "magic" or set number of factors that makes the worker an employee or an independent contractor, and no one factor stands alone in making this determination. Also, factors that are relevant in one situation may not be relevant in another.

The keys are to look at the entire relationship, consider the degree or extent of the right to direct and control, and finally, to document each of the factors used in coming up with the determination. "Independent Contractor (Self-Employed) or Employee?" https://www.irs.gov/Businesses/Small-Businesses-&-Self-Employed/Independent-Contractor-Self-Employed-or-Employee (accessed 1/23/2016).

In practice, you should bring your own laptop and desktop software; choose your own start/stop times (within reason), pay for any professional training, and maintain at least a rough schedule of work (not a work relationship that appears open-ended). As an aside, don't dilute your professional image by putting office supplies or other trivial expenses on your invoice, even if they were used on behalf of the client. You are expected to carry your own tools and buy your own supplies.

A few things to avoid

The following is a miscellaneous list of consulting icebergs that could damage your practice. The list could go on, but these are a starting point. Do not:

- Use the same invoice number twice. Most modern accounts payable systems will recognize a duplicate invoice number and kick it out. Add a random, three-digit number to your standard invoice number so that duplication is highly unlikely. When I first started my business, I submitted invoices with sequential numbers, such as 101, 102, etc. One month, when I submitted invoice number 110, my client's AP clerk keyed the invoice number as "101" instead of the correct "110." The AP manager came flying into my office – "Bill Yarberry, of all people, I can't believe you submitted a duplicate invoice." I'm fanatical about invoice accuracy, so was dumbfounded. Only later did I understand what happened. Instead of smugly informing the AP manager of my finding, I just started adding a random number at the end of my real invoice number. From that point on, my invoices followed the pattern 111-7454, 112-9334, 113-3865 and so on. It is hard to transpose a series of random numbers tacked onto the end.

- Turn in an invoice too frequently or too infrequently. Some clients will specify the frequency but usually a two-week or one-month schedule is appropriate.
- Ask the client's admin too many times about the status of your payment.
- Charge for learning skills that are standard with your business specialty. If your consultancy specializes in accounting, don't learn general accounting on the client's dime. In contrast, learning the peculiarities of a specific client's accounting-system configuration or ERP is typically billable.
- Talk about your rates, except to the individual who approves your invoice.
- Fail to back up your work and then charge the client for the time spent reconstructing the data. For less than $10/month you can use a tool like Carbonite to back up terabytes of data. I keep around 2.5 TB online. Unless there is a client initiated security restriction, keep everything—you will use it someday. "Cleaning up" your personally maintained data presumes you can see far into the future of your consulting practice (you cannot).
- Dress significantly differently from the more-senior individuals at your client's location. It's great to have high-quality clothes, but if you are the only person in the building with a necktie or wearing Prada shoes then it will be hard to blend in with the culture.
- Discuss your expense or compensation terms with anyone other than the client representative you report to. For example, some lower level employees will resent the fact that, when traveling out of town, you are permitted to bill for lunch. In their mind, you would pay for your own lunch at home, so why not when visiting the client? As your business grows, your income will exceed that of many client employees you work with. Be discrete.
- Double dip. If you are fortunate enough to have multiple projects within the same client organization, check your timesheet closely. If you charge department A for eight hours and department B for eight hours on the same day, you'll tarnish your reputation for integrity.
- Be careless with security. Conform to requirements; passwords should be at least fifteen characters long. They need not be bizarre combinations of

characters. Something easy to remember like "GreenWennieHotFrogsIce!" works. The words are unrelated.

Another iceberg you'll encounter is "calendar squeeze." This happened to me early on in my consulting practice when a client asked me to be available four months in the future. Unfortunately, I was ending a project at the time and had no other projects scheduled. What to do about four months between the time of the request and the new project? I discussed the problem with the client. Fortunately, my contact there found additional work for me and I was able to work straight through without a gap. You'll find that as your business grows, keeping your calendar full — but not too full — is a challenge. Some clients are flexible and are happy for you to work two or three days a week. Others want you to be "all in" for the duration. The key concern is that you don't get unreasonably locked in to a future date that prevents you from getting long-term work with other clients. Never stop working or looking for new work.

Seeking zero-risk and perfection

I'm sure you will read multiple books before you jump into independent consulting. You probably have hundreds of thoughts, questions, to-dos and uncertainties that run through your mind and perhaps disturb your sleep. That's a good thing. You should be reading all the books you can and letting the mistakes of others guide your way. But at some point, you'll need to take the leap. When you do, recognize that you cannot escape risk. There will be some failures. Nonetheless, follow Silicon Valley's counsel — fail fast. If you're doing a proposal, check it but get it out the door. If you're writing a blog, look at it one last time and press the enter button. The velocity of your actions drives your long-term success. Always be doing something. Your work will not be *perfect*. If it is, you are going too slow and will hurt your income stream. That doesn't mean sloppy work is acceptable but you need to recognize that at some point you'll be embarrassed by an error. For example, someone will point out that you gave monthly instead of annual numbers. In one presentation to a manufacturing prototype company, I had all the right numbers but mislabeled an Excel column. Oops. Errors like that are just going to happen unless you let perfectionism slow your work to a crawl. Fix errors quickly, keep a log of lessons learned and keep moving.

MAXIMIZE YOUR OUTPUT

Efficiency (within reason)

HOW TO GET MORE out of a day? Your priority is adequate sleep. Countless studies show the rapid falloff of productivity resulting from sleep deprivation. From an evolutionary perspective, sleep looks like a bad idea—humans become unconscious and easy meals for predators. There must be a profound need for repair and memory consolidation to justify the risk. It is all about memory consolidation; removal of the trash in our brains that comes from normal daily living; and beneficial, subconscious activities that lead to subsequent breakthrough solutions.

Beyond sleep there are plenty of incremental life changes that give you the edge in the consulting world:

- Use your electronic calendar to its fullest extent. Ensure that all your devices are linked together. Set automatic reminders, especially for those items that are important but not deadline driven. Why not have your calendar send an alert reminding you to keep up your Spanish lessons?

- Put learning tools on your mobile phone. Books and newspapers can be read while waiting in line. Since repetition is so important to learning, just a few minutes a day added to your educational schedule can make a big difference.

- Develop a follow-up system. Find a tool, such as Evernote, that will keep important information in front of you. For example, if you have a conversation with a peer about a potential but distant prospect, set a reminder note for three months into the future.

- Use a second, cheap computer, such as a Chromebook, so that you always have access to a computer. At less than $200 you can afford to have a computer in the trunk of your car, ready for any occasion. Also, your primary computer could break at the wrong time.
- Change the services that you "outsource" to fit your business schedule. If you are struggling to get started and watching your cash, then it makes sense to iron your own clothes, mow your own yard, etc. But if you have multiple clients/projects then leverage yourself by farming out as many routine tasks as possible.
- Keep your wardrobe simple.
- Deliberately surf the Internet for new topics in your subject area. It is amazing, with the power of search engines increasing exponentially, that more people don't take advantage of a daily dose of expertise. As in the Geico commercial, fifteen minutes of concentrated search can generate 15% more earnings.
- Go to an online bookstore, find books in your area, and review the table of contents. Find topics where you need more knowledge.

Self-management

Managing yourself is a big part of the job. You can't afford to get so discouraged that you stop experimenting and exploring. Just so you know they are coming, here is a short list of potential negative events you are likely to encounter, particularly during the one-to-two-year launch period:

- You will be momentarily seized with indecision. Maybe cash is running short and you need to decide whether to attend a conference with potential customers or stay where you are.
- Your lifelong insecurities, whatever they are, will loom large.
- Someone will call you out, asking why you are presenting yourself as an expert.
- Financial night terrors will disrupt your life. Unless you are starting the business with some serious money up front, relaxation is not an option. Who will pay the mortgage? Will my family slip into poverty?

A few years ago, I collaborated with an associate in responding to an RFP (request for proposal) from several firms in the nuclear industry. We assembled a great team, including nationally recognized cybersecurity specialists (one had even submitted questions for the CISSP, a prestigious security certification exam). We attended conferences, had a giant banner made, gave away a laptop in a drawing, and took key people to lunch.

Then nothing. Except that I got a call from the CIO of one of the firms, who seemed to delight in telling me why ICCM Consulting would never get the business. Presented in the guise of "helpful tips," it seemed demeaning at the time. But later I realized he was right. For that industry, generic security experience, though substantial, was not enough—we should have had far more nuclear "feet on the street" in our proposal. The point of this story is that you can do a lot of things right and still not get the business. It will happen. Expect it to happen. And then move on to the next opportunity. In my case the $8K that I lost was painful but useful intel. I never forgot the lesson.

Mind mapping

Imagine asking an expert on any subject to tell you what she knows, beginning to end. This is what early artificial intelligence developers attempted to do. I'm sure you can guess the outcome—big chunks of knowledge got left out. Unlike a sequential computer file, our brains store information more like a hologram, where details are scattered across the entire medium, not in one place and certainly not stored A to Z, in sequence. So, if you want to tap into expertise and ideas, whether your own or those of others, you need some tools to draw out concepts and stimulate creativity.

Enter mind mapping. Start with a circle in the middle and write the topic. It could be anything at any level. For example, you could mind map all the engineering inputs/outputs related to an industrial process. Other topic examples include risk reduction, strategic marketing, accounting close, and improving customer online experience. Next, draw branches out of the inner circle, showing things that affect the primary topic. In the case of risk reduction related to disaster recovery, you might have a branch for telecom redundancy and another branch for storage of data at multiple locations. Then draw smaller branches extending from the large branches until you get to some low level of detail. Details can be status, off/on, actionable recommendations, to dos, and so on.

You might ask how mind mapping is better than a structured outline. Certainly, outlines have their place. Primarily they show linear processes with multiple levels of hierarchy. Outlines work well when the subject matter is well known and various options/facts merely need to be listed. Mind maps, in contrast, are intentionally nonlinear. They facilitate brainstorming and ideation by allowing free-form structures that match thoughts or ideas that come up spontaneously in meetings or even during a self-planning session.

Mind mapping powers unstructured visualization. Pictures of objects next to branches help both presentation and retention. In fact, college students use mind maps to study for exams, finding that the combination of drawing, visualization, and connections helps them to learn. The process of drawing sometimes reveals patterns. If it looks like one branch has many subbranches, maybe there are two underlying concepts or processes that need to be broken out.

The illustration below shows a partial view of a mind map for layered cybersecurity. Note the use of pictures to emphasize concepts.

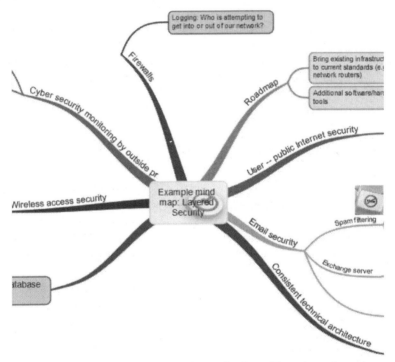

Mind map for layered security (not all sections shown)

Outsourcing to expand your day

You don't need to do it all. Depending on cash flow, there are many functions that can be conveniently outsourced. For example, you could use one of the many online boutique firms to write regular blogs and other content for you. Online ads, search-engine optimization, and a host of other services are readily available. Upwork.com is an example of firms that provide such services. If time is your critical resource, outsource tasks not core to your practice. This advice is mostly applicable after your first year or eighteen months, when your practice is firmly established and cash is not as critical.

Because clients and projects do not arrive in your queue in a steady stream, you'll almost certainly be overwhelmed at some point. That is when your peer contacts are invaluable. If the client wants forty hours a week that you don't have to give, then try to bring in someone you trust and supply the resource with minimal markup. To the extent possible, be a one-stop shop for your clients. Of course, you do want to stay within your expertise enough to evaluate any work done under your oversight.

Keeping a business journal

Keeping a business journal becomes increasingly important as you develop long-term relationships with multiple clients. Your journal can be any format and certainly does not need to be polished; it's only for your reference. Record as much as you can and as fast as you can. I use a Word document with an entry each business day. Attaching that document to an Evernote or OneNote note ensures that it is backed up and searchable.

While a paper journal will work, digital is better for searching (some tools will recognize handwriting). The journal will help you consolidate your memories and find key facts relevant to your clients. After you've gotten the five-digit check for a successful project, maybe you take a three-week cruise of the Greek islands. It is helpful to have your journal handy when you get back. Research shows that most people believe their memory for detail is better than it is. Example entries that go into your business journal include:
- Meeting times and results or link to minutes.
- Names of people you meet during the day and their positions.
- Facts about processes, products, and ongoing projects.
- File names of important documents.

81

- Rough, back of the envelope sketches of processes, potential approaches and complex ideas. Visuals, however crude, are excellent mnemonics.

Computer-file discipline

A real benefit of having a long-term client is that you can be the document repository of last resort. Your customer will have thousands of Word, Excel, and PowerPoint files, so she "has" what she is looking for but it is buried. Ideally, you have a superior filing method and can find a document based on a vague description—"It had something to do with Fred and incident response. Seems like it was three years ago."

So how do you develop such a filing system? There's no one answer. Some consultants have intensely categorical minds and can arrange documents in consistent and meaningful folder structures. I cannot. My method is to retain anything of potential value using an immensely long file name, such as "Incident response draft reviewed by Fred Young. Freita initially contributed. Meeting held in 4th floor conference room. Topic related to the GG&C initiative.docx" Windows, for example, will allow at least 255 characters in the file name. Windows searches allow you to query any part of the file name. If you need to send the file to the client after retrieving it, save it under a shorter name. With processor speeds and disk IO getting better every year, a whole disk drive search is practical.

When it comes to computer-file discipline, the gorilla in the room is backup. If you have a single document with $15,000 worth of consulting hours behind it, you not only need multiple copies but you need multiple versions stored in separate locations, including online. It happens repeatedly—the same file name is used for both the active document and backup. Later it is discovered that an error(s) was made inside the document and that error has been propagated to the backups. Use versions. I've had projects where I saved one-hundred versions of a key document. Don't rely completely on an automated versioning system like SharePoint. Things happen. As Andy Grove of Intel famously remarked, "Only the paranoid survive."

THE FUTURE OF INDEPENDENT CONSULTING

Coming up soon

AS AN INDEPENDENT CONSULTANT, you are on the right side of history. We are in the middle of a dramatic, advanced industrial revolution where everything you do is accelerated with greater scope and more system impact. Every year there will be exponential increases in computing power and vast increases in data, as well as improved and easy-to-use analytics. In 2017 Gartner noted that more devices were connected to the Internet than the world's population.[10]

Your productivity can continue to grow regardless of whether you choose to remain a sole proprietor or hire employees. With virtual assistants of all sorts and tools we haven't even dreamed of, you can be as big a virtual firm as you like. Capital drives what organizations can do, but increasingly human talent counts for long-term profitability. With your specialized skills and constant education, you'll be in a perfect spot to offer complex and innovative services to your clients. After the initial startup, you will worry more about how much time you must commit to business than you worry about acquiring new clients. As of this writing about 30% of the world uses

---

[10] Tung, Liam. "IoT Devices Will Outnumber the World's Population This Year for the First Time." *ZDNet*, ZDNet, 13 Feb. 2017, www.zdnet.com/article/iot-devices-will-outnumber-the-worlds-population-this-year-for-the-first-time/.

social media. In absolute terms this is a gigantic number and will only increase. As so many people come online, their ability to reach you in a variety of ways—the number of sales channels—will grow.

You will delight your clients by continually improving your understanding of what they want and by enhancing your own services. As so much work becomes collaborative, your communication skills will serve as the oil on the water to make projects run smoothly. So yes, you'll need to spend a significant percentage of your own budget on technology. Software, hardware, and communication services will be your factory. You will be ever more reachable by those who need you. Collaboration tools will steadily improve.

Who knows what will be important? Smart watches will get smarter; virtual/augmented reality will move to the realm of everyday use, and you may find yourself doing international business by means of your consulting firm's avatar. Many firms are working feverishly on the real opportunities that will arise when space travel becomes cheap. Bitcoin or, more accurately, the blockchain technology underpinning it, is poised to dramatically speed and reduce the cost of transitions. The concept of distributed trust, where no central authority is needed to intercede between parties who do not know each other, has many applications.

On average, this new world will include shorter projects and more-dispersed activities. Even though I stress that personal contact is important, there is a push to impersonal contact due to worldwide availability of services. This of course means that you need to have your online etiquette format honed to a perfect edge.

Superfast broadband, both wireline and wireless, is coming — more Skype and less travel. Baby boomers are rapidly retiring and there is a shortage of skilled labor across the board. Deloitte Consulting reports that on average it takes industry more than 90 days to recruit highly skilled workers. This means that if you are already known, you are more likely to get the work.

The concept of fungibility is as important in the future as it is now. It means that you can be inserted in processes where there are gaps in your client's knowledge base, skill set, or simply resource availability. We don't know how some things will affect the future of consulting. For example, firms such as Airbnb and Uber have taken advantage of the sharing economy to take a serious bite out of existing capital-based industries.

By 2020 it is estimated that there will be more than 200 billion "things" connected to the Internet. These connections will be for everything from smart lawn mowers to context aware cubicles. Directed by smart cloud applications, these connected devices offer sophisticated services. As your practice grows, knowing more about these trends is critical. Clients expect you to see a little further down the road than anyone else.

Today the large consulting firms are very much like a pyramid, with the senior partners on top earning very high salaries and associates at the bottom earning considerably less. Associates are nonetheless billed out to the client at hefty margins. That model may change because clients are increasingly unwilling to pay to get associates up to speed. This may be a problem for the industry and society, but it certainly is something you can take advantage of. As an independent consultant you have no "partner tax."

There has been a discussion for many years about whether the work-from-home trend will continue. While you can never get away from face time, when you get busy and must juggle schedules then remote work is what you need. Expect to work an increasing amount of your time in a home office as your client base expands. Even with self-driving cars, it is difficult to get to three clients in the same day. One of my associates, a private plane enthusiast and pilot, told me that Houston to Austin in an hour is a reasonable flight time. I doubt this option is viable for my practice, but if you are already a small plane pilot, it could be practical. My guess is that regardless of technology, most consultants cannot "swivel their head" fast enough to do well in more than three client meetings a day.

The next decade

All other things being equal, the faster you learn the more money you will make. This is both bad and good news. The need for learning new, domain-specific knowledge directly relates to depreciation of old knowledge. The future and the profits go to independent consultants who are the most efficient learners. Every year artificial intelligence (AI) systems do more work in specialized niches. Jetliners are in part flown by AI, although a full human crew is still required. Self-driving cars and long haul trucks will slowly take over the world's highways. This becomes your personal race—to move up the complexity/efficiency curve, discarding ever more of your rote services, and replacing them with creative solutions. To take a line from Star Trek, resistance to AI is futile. Just stay one step ahead.

In the 1980s IBM lost the desktop computer race because its senior executives could not bring themselves to cannibalize mainframe sales to promote the PC. The willingness to "eat your own babies" applies to consulting as well. If you are doing X for your client using existing methods but can bring new technology or processes to bear for a tenth the cost, do it. It may cost billable hours in the short term, but you'll stay competitive and sought after.

Changes in technology, communications, and processes are happening at an exponential rate. This means that up-to-date knowledge and deep expertise are ever more in demand.

CONCLUSION

W HEN LOOKING FOR GUIDANCE in the early years of my practice I found books about structure, taxes, and marketing. What I didn't find was a book that mimicked a private conversation between me (contemplating an independent practice) and a close friend who had been in the business several years. What is important? What should I know that no one will tell me? My inability to find these fundamentals motivated me to write this book. If just one idea helps you attract a new client, save time, delight the person who brought you into a company or avoid a costly faux pas, then I'm happy with the result. I want to get you closer to your goal of independence and financial success.

If nothing else, we've learned from psychological research over the last hundred years that our behavior and decision making are determined by subconscious and often emotional motivations. To be successful you must sense: a) what is meant rather than what is said, b) the hidden/informal rules, and c) the three parts of customer need: the business organization; the people formally assigned to positions in that company; and the subconscious drivers that dwell in the heart of each person you work with.

In these pages we talked about:
- Both the risks and security of independent consulting.
- Why your services are needed.
- Money matters.
- Potential pricing structures.
- Consultant's tool kit.
- Taxes and insurance.
- Marketing, business development, branding.
- Templates, read-to-modify documents.
- Skill sets.
- Avoidance strategies so you don't shoot your own foot.
- Outsourcing overflow work.
- Client relationships and dogfights.
- Thoughts on near-term futures.

To sum it all up: **You can do this.** You don't need to be beautiful, any particular age, a great speaker, or from a sophisticated part of the country. What you do need is basic competence in your field, a continued willingness to learn, flexibility, high sensitivity to the client, hard work, and patience.

Thank you for taking the time to read this short book. Much more could be written, but I hope this gives you some insight into the risks and rewards of the independent consultant's life. I welcome questions, corrections, general comments, or suggestions for other topics. Send to: byarberry@iccmconsulting.net. I am also happy to send you a free mock business plan which can be used as a model for any business (it is not specifically for consulting).

* * *

If you have found this book useful, please leave a review on Amazon. It helps me and it helps other readers searching for guidance on independent consulting. Best wishes for your continued success.

Bill Yarberry, CPA
Houston, Texas USA
February 10, 2018

APPENDICES

The independent consultant's canned toolbox

Y OU ARE EXPECTED to know the standard consultant playbook/toolbox. Some of these methods are obsolete or perhaps primitive; however, your client may have developed techniques ten or twenty years ago. On the other hand, some may be looking for the technique of the day. You need to have at least familiarity with these techniques and stay on top of them throughout your consulting career. The list below is in no particular order or age of introduction. There are endless varieties on the Internet, so use these as a starting point for further research.

Detection of errors, anomalies, and data/text behaviors of interest

Eventually nearly everyone in the consulting business will be asked to "sniff around" a system, records, logs or other information repositories. In some cases, this will be a formal request and a routine part of the job (e.g., substantive testing in audit). At other times, the client may just want a casual look. A client in Detroit asked me to review a report of carrier billings for one quarter. Within ten minutes I found $25K of duplicate bills. The vendor, AT&T, had been set up twice by accounts payable, once as AT&T and once as A.T.T. For another client I performed a test I thought was almost unnecessary—looking for any company assets with a net value less than zero. I found two.

The following list of potential tests are merely suggestions and a starting point for your subject area of expertise. For example, consultants in mechanical engineering/safety may review logs for evidence of pitted cylinder rods and worn cylinder packings. A nonprofit consultant may review board minutes for the presence or absence of specific officer compensation resolutions. The checklists will be dramatically different in detail across industries, but logic applies across the board.

Tests for anomalies:

- Duplication of key information, such as invoice number, specific codes, and other information where each observation should be unique.
- Duplication of precise numbers that should slightly vary. This may or may not be an error. For example, when a purity test for lead in water results in a value of 15.77386 ppb five times in a row, the results are suspicious. Precise testing typically shows a pattern of variation around a central number.
- Large number of exact entries (e.g., rounded-off dollars rather than dollars and cents).
- Monotonically (always) increasing or decreasing over time. If a client has an initiative to reduce scrap and records six months of data, it is not reasonable that the number would decrease each day. Like going on a successful diet, while the total may decrease over weeks or months, each day will vary up or down.
- Unexplained gaps in records. If a week is missing out of three years of data, further investigation may be warranted.
- Reasonable consistency. Huge swings, as increases or decreases, may indicate bad record keeping.
- Events or transactions at odd hours.
- Application of Benford's law. The description of Benford's law and application is outside the scope of this book. If you suspect that records have been humanly altered rather than "naturally" generated from, say, retail sales, a Benford law analysis may be warranted. The first two digits of unaltered numbers show a pattern in which there are more digits close to "00" than "99." The IRS has used this technique to identify tax fraud.
- Use text analysis tools to identify specific words, word frequencies, and words of interest that occur within a "distance" of four or five words from each other. This typically requires software beyond the usual Microsoft or Google Desktop, but may be appropriate if it is an important project and you are looking for specific occurrences. For example, if a plant manager has given a vendor an excessive number of steep discounts, a text analysis of all emails may suggest an unusual proximity of the vendor name and the word "discount."
- Merge independent files that should contain common information. For example, invoices should not be made out to customers that are not found on

the customer master. An even more relevant example is a payables invoice where no comparable vendor is found on the master.

- Sort numbers to show the largest and smallest values. Inspect for abnormalities.
- Sample populations and drill down to look for abnormalities (unstructured).
- Summarize and graph by key information such as product type, geographic location, organizational number, or other key categorization values. Examine values that are extreme.
- Look at ratios. For example, the ratio of sales returns to sales should be roughly consistent over time and across organizational units. Deviations could indicate fraud, inefficiency, or a broken process.
- Review standard performance measures.
- Age any assets so that you can review over time. An excessive concentration in older time periods may indicate inefficiency or a deeper problem.
- Look for spikes of numbers just below any psychological cutoff. For example, if the requirement for expense item documentation is exactly $30, review the number of records that are bunched up just below $30, such as $29.99.
- Look for negative numbers where all should be positive, and positive numbers where all should be negative. For example, the net value of an asset should never be negative.
- Take the logarithm of values of interest and manually look for odd patterns. Excel uses the "log()" function to generate the logarithm. For example, log(100) equals 2.

An example of a consulting agreement

Note: this example is for illustrative purposes only. **It does not represent legal advice.** Please see your attorney when creating your actual contracts with clients.

January 15, 2018

Mr. Jonathan Doe
Director — Regulatory Compliance
Most Excellent Manufacturing, Inc. [11]
3811 Galaxy Street
Houston, Texas 77987

Dear Mr. Doe:

This Consulting Agreement ("Agreement") shall be effective as of January 15, 2018 ("Effective Date") by and between ICCM Consulting and Most Excellent Manufacturing, Inc.

Introductory Statement:
This Agreement confirms our previous discussions in which ICCM Consulting, LLC ("ICCM") proposed to assist Most Excellent Manufacturing, Inc. (the "Client" or MEM) with a series of internal process, procedure documentation, and risk assessment projects in connection with Client's Sarbanes-Oxley compliance program. This Agreement, when accepted, shall comprise an overall framework enabling ICCM's participation in any number of such projects, at the discretion of Most Excellent Manufacturing's management.

ICCM reserves the right to advise clients and potential clients with whom we have worked on these projects for Most Excellent Manufacturing, Inc.; however, the terms and conditions of this Consulting Agreement shall remain confidential between the parties hereto.

Scope of Work
The general scope of this Agreement involves ICCM providing documentation and risk-assessment services and assistance to MEM on a project basis, as provided herein. Such assistance could include, but not necessarily be limited to, conducting reviews of

---

[11] A fictitious company.

appropriate books, records, and other documentation maintained by MEM or any party doing business with MEM; interviewing MEM employees, former employees, or representatives of outside firms or other parties designated by MEM; the collection and collation of relevant documents and related materials; and the preparation of transaction flowcharts and documentation or policy and procedure narratives. If so requested, assistance could also include the preparation of one or more analyses or memoranda in connection with such findings as ICCM may make relative to its involvement with regard to the projects.

Our work products are intended solely for the information and use of MEM's management and Board of Directors and should not be used for any other purpose.

MEM's auditors and regulators may be provided with a copy of any work product in connection with fulfilling their respective responsibilities.

Proposed Project Team

This proposal is issued by ICCM Consulting, LLC ("ICCM"), a sole member limited liability company owned by William Yarberry.

Mr. Yarberry will be the primary individual assigned to these projects. Subject to the approval of MEM Internal Audit management, Mr. Yarberry may be assisted by ICCM associates, as required.

Fees and Expenses

ICCM's fees will be billed to MEM at the rate of $120.00 per hour, plus any out-of-pocket expenses incurred. All travel time shall be compensated at the specified hourly rate, but not to exceed three hours in a twenty-four-hour period. Travel to and from ICCM's offices to MEM's main office shall not be charged.

We will invoice you on a biweekly basis, with the first invoice dated as of February 15, 2018. Such invoices shall reflect the number of hours charged by us during the period covered by the invoice. Travel expenses within the Houston, Texas metropolitan area will be billed at $0.53 per mile, plus tolls and parking, if any. Where out-of-town or out-of-country travel is required, we will bill you for meals, lodging, transportation, and incidental expenses on an actual-costs basis.

All ICCM invoices are due and payable without delay upon presentation.

General Provisions

ICCM shall not bear any responsibility whatsoever for any actions taken or not taken by MEM, its Board of Directors, or its management with respect to any project. MEM stipulates that any and all actions, including any decision not to take action, will be based on its own assessment of the project(s) and ICCM shall not be held liable for any outcome resulting therefrom.

This proposal presumes the full support and cooperation of all appropriate MEM personnel and departments. It is expected that this will include several key people making themselves available for whatever amounts of time are required, and that secretarial and clerical support and appropriate work space will be made available to project team members working on site. MEM agrees to work with us on a collaborative basis, including an open dialogue and exchange of information concerning each project. MEM will furnish or communicate to ICCM documents or information that MEM has obtained and developed or will develop so that we are, and can remain, fully apprised.

MEM shall be responsible for scoping and defining each project and authorizing ICCM and its team to participate in or conduct the project on MEM's behalf. Further, MEM shall be responsible for arranging appropriate access to, as examples and without limitation, all relevant locations, facilities, and personnel, as well as the relevant books, records, financial statements, contracts, and other documents. Such access may include providing appropriate letters of introduction from MEM to individuals and institutions necessary to the project.

It should be recognized that projects of the nature contemplated will not necessarily result in the discovery of every possible error, irregularity, or illegal act, including fraud or defalcation that may exist, nor the implementation of all necessary actions, corrective or otherwise. However, ICCM will inform MEM Internal Audit management of any such matters that come to our attention. Furthermore, while observations and recommendations will be reported, the consideration and adoption thereof is the responsibility of the appropriate MEM management. Because of the nature of these projects. ICCM's work will only include such documentation and risk-assessment work as is assigned, and will not include detailed testing or verification of records, representations, or assertions unless we are directed to do so by MEM Internal Audit management.

MEM acknowledges that any advice we may give or conclusions that we may reach could be modified or reversed, depending on the existence of facts and circumstances unknown to us.

All notes, memoranda, analyses, studies, other documents, and other information prepared or communicated by ICCM in the course of performance of this engagement will be solely for MEM's benefit and at MEM's direction. We agree that any information that is designated as confidential, nonpublic information that we receive from MEM in connection with this Agreement or these projects will be maintained as confidential by us, using due care and the normal procedures we employ to protect such confidential information. Analyses, memoranda, and documentation, if any, prepared for each assigned task will become the property of MEM and will remain confidential documents.

Upon termination of our employment hereunder we will, without regard to the time, manner, or cause of said termination, surrender to MEM all original lists, books, records, or other material of or in connection with the affairs of MEM, and will return to MEM forthwith all property of whatever nature belonging to MEM.

Notwithstanding the above, our right to prepare or obtain information (including the copying or acceptance of MEM- or third-party-prepared materials such as lists, books, records, or other materials, whether printed or copied) on or related to MEM or third party of any nature whatsoever necessary to the conduct of our engagement with MEM, including background materials, and to retain and use such materials (collectively constituting our "working papers") as part of our professional practice, subject to the confidentiality terms and conditions hereof, are expressly acknowledged and agreed to. Nothing in this Agreement shall serve to limit our use of ideas, concepts, and industry knowledge, among other information, in providing services to our clients.

ICCM does not guarantee any specific outcome, recommendation, or conclusion. All such outcomes, recommendations, and conclusions shall be independently arrived at by us, without regard to whether they are favorable or unfavorable to MEM or any third party.

It is understood and agreed that the relationship of ICCM and its officers. employees, and associates with MEM are those of independent contractors and not those of employees. Therefore MEM shall not have any worker's compensation liability to any of us. We shall not represent to any person that we have any relationship with MEM other than that of consultants.

Should this engagement involve any officer, employee, or associate of ICCM presenting testimony or reports to a government agency or representative or to a court, such testimony shall become the subject of a separate engagement letter.

The term of this Agreement shall be indefinite; however, either MEM or ICCM may elect to terminate this Agreement at any time by written notice to the other. The nondisclosure requirements and limitations on the use of information furnished to ICCM or developed for MEM by ICCM during the course of this engagement shall survive such termination. Any accrued fees and expenses due ICCM shall be immediately due and payable upon termination. Notwithstanding anything to the contrary, MEM's obligation to pay all fees and expenses incurred by ICCM shall not terminate until paid in full.

This agreement shall be construed under and in accordance with the laws of the state of Texas. Venue for any action brought under or in connection with this Agreement shall be in Harris County, Texas.

In case any one or more of the provisions of this Agreement shall for any reason be held invalid, illegal, or unenforceable in any respect, such invalidity, illegality, or unenforceability shall not affect any other provision thereof; and this Agreement shall be construed as if such invalid, illegal, or unenforceable provision had never been contained herein.

TO THE FULLEST EXTENT PERMITTED UNDER APPLICABLE LAW. ICCM AGREES TO DEFEND, INDEMNIFY, AND SAVE MEM HARMLESS FROM ANY LIABILITIES, CLAIMS, OR DEMANDS (INCLUDING THE COSTS, EXPENSES, AND ATTORNEYS' AND EXPERTS' FEES ON ACCOUNT THEREOF) THAT MAY BE MADE (A) BY ANYONE FOR INJURIES TO PERSONS OR DAMAGE TO PROPERTY, INCLUDING THEFT, RESULTING FROM ICCM'S ACTS OR OMISSIONS OR THOSE OF PERSONS EMPLOYED BY ICCM; OR (B) BY PERSONS EMPLOYED BY ICCM OR BY ANY SUBCONTRACTORS USED BY ICCM, FOR INJURIES OR DAMAGES CLAIMED UNDER WORKERS COMPENSATION OR SIMILAR ACT. IT IS EXPRESSLY UNDERSTOOD AND STIPULATED BY THE PARTIES THAT ICCM SHALL BE RESPONSIBLE FOR ANY AND ALL FEES, COSTS, AND EXPENSES RELATED TO THE DEFENSE OF MEM, OR ANY OF ITS RELATED OR AFFILIATED ENTITIES, AGAINST ANY SUCH LIABILITY, CLAIM, OR DEMAND SHOULD MEM SO REQUEST. MEM SHALL BE ENTITLED TO SELECT COUNSEL AND EXPERTS OF ITS CHOICE AND IN ITS SOLE AND EXCLUSIVE DISCRETION. THE INDEMNIFICATION RIGHTS, DUTIES, AND OBLIGATIONS CREATED HEREUNDER ARE INTENDED TO THE FULLEST EXTENT PERMITTED BY APPLICABLE LAW. IN PARTICULAR, ICCM HEREBY AGREES TO BE DIRECTLY RESPONSIBLE TO THIRD PARTIES FOR ANY DAMAGES, CLAIMS, DEMANDS, AND THE LIKE FOR OR RELATING TO ICCM'S SERVICES HEREUNDER, AS WELL AS ANY DAMAGE TO PERSONAL AND/OR REAL PROPERTY, NEGLIGENCE, GROSS NEGLIGENCE, OR WILLFUL MISCONDUCT RELATING TO THIS AGREEMENT AND/OR THE WORK PERFORMED HEREUNDER OR IN CONNECTION HEREWITH.

ICCM further assumes responsibility and liability for any claims or actions based on or arising out of injuries, including death, to persons or damages to or destruction of property sustained or alleged to have been sustained in connection with or to have arisen out of or incidental to the performance of this contract by ICCM, its agents and employees, and its subcontractors, their agents and employees, including claims or actions founded in whole or in part on the negligence or alleged negligence of MEM, MEM's affiliates, representatives, or the employees, agents, invitees, or licensees thereof. ICCM further agrees to defend, indemnify, and hold harmless MEM and its affiliates, representatives, and the employees, agents, invitees, and licensees thereof in respect of any such matters and agrees to defend any claim or suit or action brought against MEM, MEM's affiliates, representatives, and the employees, agents, invitees, and licensees thereof.

This agreement constitutes the sole and only agreement of the parties hereto with respect to the subject matter hereof and supersedes any prior understandings, representations, statements, or agreements between the parties. Any change, amendment or modification of this Agreement must be evidenced in writing and executed by both parties.

Please confirm your acceptance of this Agreement on the terms herein set forth by signing and returning the original of this proposal to us, retaining a copy for your files.

We are pleased to present this proposal to Most Excellent Manufacturing, Inc. , and we look forward to a long and mutually beneficial relationship. Please do not hesitate to call on us whenever we can be of assistance.

Very truly yours,

ICCM CONSULTING, LLC

— — — — — — — — — — — — — —

William A. Yarberry, Jr, CPA

CONFIRMED AND ACCEPTED as of the day and year first above written:
Most Excellent Manufacturing, Inc.

— — — — — — — — — — — — — —

By: Jonathan Doe, Director—Regulatory Compliance

Graphical toolkits

Mind map

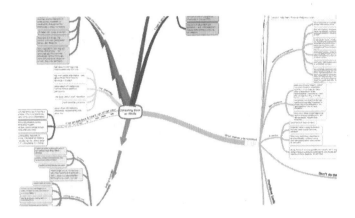

Porter's value chain model

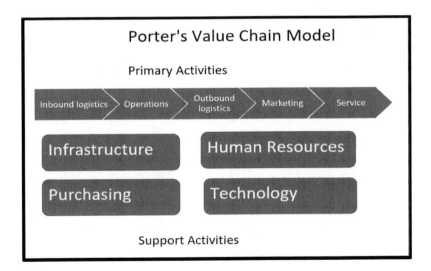

Pestle analysis

P - Politics

L - Legal

E - Economy

Pestle Analysis

E - Environment

S - Social

T - Technology

Word cloud

As a graphic to add color to a presentation, you can use the free Word Cloud generator https://www.wordclouds.com/. Using any document you choose, the website will generate a word cloud based on the contents of the document. The most prominent words are larger than less-frequent words; a variety of styles and colors are available. The following is a word cloud generated from an early version of this book.

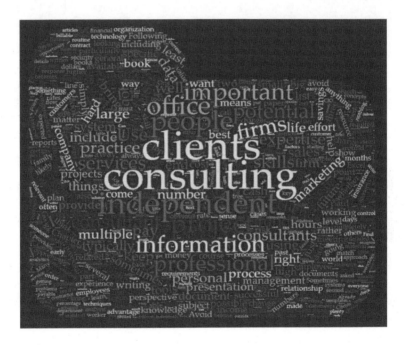

Artifacts from the consulting business

Example response letter after verbal go-ahead from a client

November 1, 2017

Mr. Francon Calcington
XYZ Corp, Inc.
Apex Group
Houston, TX 77001

Dear Francon,

I was delighted to receive your email last week. It looks like an interesting project and is a good fit with my background. As I mentioned in our conversation, I worked for Elizabeth Rexington's compliance/audit liaison/security group at QRS Services for approximately four months in the fall of 2016.

I hope that the attached SOW[12] accurately reflects our conversation. I used XYZ's SOW format. I'm not sure whether XYZ-West has a similar master services agreement that I need to sign, so I left that part in red lettering and with question marks. The one I signed in 2015 may still apply.

Assuming you find my background acceptable, I'll make the changes you suggest to the SOW and proceed with any other required paperwork. It would be great to work with Alfonzo again, and I probably know a few of the others at the data center.

Thanks for your flexibility on the financial terms. I look forward to working with you.

Best regards,

Bill

---

[12] Author's note: SOW is a statement of work, which includes detailed descriptions of the work to be performed, project reporting, due dates, and other specific information related to the project.

Example letter to potential client after a sales presentation

Mr. Al Thermopylae
Chief Financial Officer
ACE Thermal Insulators, Inc.
2825 Thrall Drive
Houston, TX 77042

Dear Al,

John and I appreciate the opportunity to propose the attached security/SOD consulting project for ACE Thermal Insulators.

The meetings with Jim, Amir, and others at ACE were most helpful. Hearing the concerns and objectives firsthand allowed us to put together a phased project. Our intent is to enable a faster, more-secure rollout of the Adiabatic system to additional users.

If you have any questions or concerns please let us know. We're excited about the opportunity and ready to work!

Best regards,

William A. Yarberry, Jr, CPA
Principal Consultant
ICCM Consulting, LLC

Note to reader: for this project I teamed up with an SME –(subject matter expert) to deliver services on a system in which I had no expertise.

Formal engagement letter

Lengthy, detailed engagement letters are more common for large projects and organizations with a precisely defined set of project procedures. A similar but less-detailed letter would be appropriate for smaller, more informal organizations. Either way, you need something to document the scope of the work. Without an engagement letter, a misunderstanding about deliverables could tarnish the relationship. To use an obvious example, consulting and recommendations should be clearly separated from implementation of those recommendations. Either combine them into one proposal with sections clearly defined and costed, or create two proposals.

You should have an attorney prepare the terms and conditions for your first large client project. After that you can usually copy all or some portion of the engagement letter for other clients. The following is intended to be illustrative only, and may not be appropriate for your particular engagement.

March 31, 2016

Mr. Thomas Highton
Director, Internal Audit
Aurora II Mining Corporation[13]
3989 Leeson Avenue
Austin, Texas 78682

Subject: Telecommunications Cost Management Practices Review

Dear Mr. Highton:

This letter confirms that Aurora II Mining Corporation ("AMC") has retained ICCM Consulting, LLC ("ICCM") to provide the services (the "Services") set out below. The purpose of this letter, which incorporates the attached Terms and Conditions, is to confirm our understanding of the terms of the engagement. This letter constitutes the entire agreement between the parties with respect to ICCM's performance of the Services.

Scope

---

[13] A fictitious company.

Based on knowledge of current operational processes, Internal Audit believes opportunities exist for process improvement and reductions in telecommunications costs within the existing telecom architecture. Process improvements may be necessary due to significant telecommunications growth and staff changes experienced by the company. These potentially excessive costs can arise from a variety of sources, including but not limited to deficiencies in cost-monitoring systems, excess/premature capacity, weaknesses in termination and authorization procedures, billing errors, suboptimal rate plans, and inappropriate telecommunications assets.

In addition to cost management, AMC is also interested in the security of the voice communications network (specifically VoIP and voicemail controls). AMC has requested that ICCM conduct a limited assessment of voice communications security, as well as cost management practices, processes, and controls for a representative sample of telecommunications services.

Approach

Our approach, outlined below, is designed to reduce your risk of excess telecommunications costs and security breaches by identifying specific areas in which a subsequent review across AMC's entire telecommunications network will provide a high payback. We will interview selected staff responsible for the telecommunications security, procurement, processes, and cost-management functions to understand AMC's telecommunications activities and to identify control points within your current processes. We will compare these results of our data gathering to telecommunications best practices to identify areas that have higher risks and merit an additional review to bring their risk profile in line with your expectations. We will work with your telecommunications management team to identify a representative sample of organizational units (offices, manufacturing facilities, other departments) that will provide the detailed information necessary to develop our recommendations. Within the representative sample, our assessment will include high-level coverage of the following areas of your telecommunications function:

Cost Management

Telecommunications services procurement process, including but not limited to:

- Requirements specification and justification
- Contract preparation

- Service provisioning and service validation
- Contract compliance
- General policies and procedures

Calling cards
- Authorization for setup and exception events
- Termination procedures
-
- Audio conferencing
- Use of volume discounts
- Bridge only versus fully costed (including LD minutes) usage
- Cost-saving potential for in-house audio conferencing

Capacity planning and monitoring
- Incremental provisioning (premature versus insufficient increase)
- Consideration of alternatives (e.g., asymmetric PVCs for frame relay)
- Build-out provisioning (new offices, floors, etc.)

Video conferencing
- Utilization of facilities
- Setup/teardown controls
- Bridge/CODEC costs

High-level review of current billing self-audit process. Functional areas include but are not limited to:

- Telecom invoices
- Customer service record USOC codes and related charges
-
- IXC review, including comparison of contract rates with actual charges for all usage-sensitive calls by service and type
- Contracted or lowest tariff rate with actual billed rate
- 800 number usage (particularly low usage)
- Customer-carrier correspondence (to verify, for example, that disconnect orders were properly implemented)
- Unnecessary LEC and IXC circuits, including access circuits
- Charges for LEC premium services, such as "emergency interrupt"
- Evidence of "slamming" and "cramming"
- IXC charges on LEC bills
- Appropriate "PICC" codes

- Call detail, if available (review for anomalies)

Chargeback for Services

Coverage (scope of telecom chargeback/call accounting within AMC)
- PBXs and geographic locations included
- Telecommunications functions (e.g., calling cards, cellular, equipment)
- Hierarchies of reporting
- Capture profile—incoming, outgoing, internal, local, long distance, private line

Financial reporting and budget variances

Scope of telecom chargeback

Charge algorithm/methodologies

Technical reporting architecture (paper-based, intranet, etc.)
- Real time or off-line
- Distribution and reporting frequency
- Reporting to cost-center managers and line management accountability

Hardware
- Polling and transmission from multiple sites (e.g., buffer boxes)
- Chargeback backup systems and redundancy requirements
- Inventory management; day-to-day operations
- Circuit analysis (e.g., T1, T3, DS3 usage)
- Gap analysis (missing data)
- Toll fraud and security alerts
- Historical retention of call data
- Analog line inventory

—— additional content deleted ——————-

Information Gathering and Process Documentation

ICCM will further its understanding of the AMC telecommunications environment through the following activities:

- Conduct interviews to gather an understanding of telecommunications cost management and security processes. Groups to be interviewed will be defined with the assistance of AMC, but may include:
- Operations
- IT Strategic Planning
- End users of telecommunications services
- IT Finance
- Work with AMC Internal Audit and Telecommunications group to identify a representative sample of organizational units for detailed review
- Use electronic data across the entire organization, where practical within the time limitations of the engagement, to identify potential excess costs and trends that merit management attention
- Survey selected groups/users with advance approval from AMC
- Identify one representative PBX and voice-mail system for security analysis at an intermediate level of detail (i.e., including both control review and examination of specific security related parameters)
- Identify one or two small to medium departments for a detailed chargeback/telecom cost-accounting analysis
- Top down/every nth sample selection of call detail from one PBX
- Top down/every nth sample selection of telecom vendor payments from the accounts payable system for one or two business units

Deliverables

The deliverables for this engagement include a presentation and summation of our findings that will be delivered to AMC Internal Audit management. Specifically, the deliverables will contain the following:

- An executive summary of the project results that can be presented and distributed to key management at AMC. This summary will include a description of the work performed, documentation of cost-improvement opportunities, security risks identified, and suggested procedural improvements.
- Based on identified cost saving opportunities in the areas sampled, provide an approximation of savings if the recommendations were implemented across all AMC business units.
- A detailed listing of findings in the standard AMC Internal Audit format (process, objective, business risk, and control).

- An approximate breakdown of telecommunications expenses by function for management review. This analysis will be obtained by statistical sampling and manual assignment of expense categories.

ICCM's deliverables are solely for AMC management's and/or board of directors' use and benefit. They may not be distributed to any other party without our written consent. We may provide oral advice in conjunction with this engagement, and such advice cannot be attributed to ICCM unless, after you fully consider it, we confirm such advice in writing.

AMC responsibilities

The overall definition and scope of the work to be performed and its adequacy in addressing AMC's needs are AMC's responsibility. ICCM Consulting, LLC will rely on AMC to meet its responsibilities as set forth in the attached Terms and Conditions. We will rely on AMC to provide access to systems, documents, and personnel as required. Our fee estimate presented herein takes into account the agreed-on level of preparation and assistance from AMC personnel. We will advise management on a timely basis if you do not provide the required information or resources, or should any other circumstances arise that may cause actual time to exceed our estimate. AMC personnel agree to work with ICCM to a mutually agreeable conclusion should such circumstances arise.

It is agreed that responsibility for the implementation of actions identified in the course of this assignment rests with AMC, its management, and employees.

Resources performing the work

William Yarberry and one to two designated subcontractors will be performing the work. AMC is welcome to review the work qualifications of any subcontractors. If AMC finds such subcontractors unsuitable, ICCM will use alternates approved by AMC.

Timetable

We are ready to begin this engagement within one week of your approval. We expect to complete all work and provide deliverables within five weeks of starting fieldwork for this engagement.

Achieving this timetable is subject to, among other things, full cooperation from AMC personnel, including providing necessary information, timely responses to our inquiries, and the necessary active participation from appropriate personnel.

Fees

Fees are estimated to be $65,000. In addition, out-of-pocket expenses will be billed at cost (estimated $5,500). Such expenses will include all travel, lodging, subsistence, and an allocation of office charges in support of our services including computer usage, telephone, facsimile transmission, postage, photo reproduction, and similar expenses. The estimated professional-services fees provided above are valid for only thirty days from the date of this correspondence.

If during the course of our work it appears that our fee will exceed this estimate we will provide prompt notice to AMC. ICCM Consulting, LLC will not undertake work that is beyond the nature and scope of that which is contemplated in this letter without AMC's prior approval.

An initial bill of 10 percent of total fees will be issued upon start date, and subsequent billings will be made every four weeks. Invoices are due within fourteen days of receipt.

ICCM Consulting, LLC is pleased to have the opportunity to continue our relationship with AMC and appreciate your interest in our telecommunications consulting capabilities. If you have any questions about the contents of this letter please discuss them with us. If the services outlined herein are in accordance with AMC's requirements and the terms described are acceptable, please sign one copy of this letter in the space provided and return it to me.

Very truly yours,

William A. Yarberry, Jr., CPA
Principal Consultant
ICCM Consulting, LLC

Bill Yarberry, CPA

The services and terms set forth in this letter, including the attached Terms and Conditions, are agreed to.

Aurora II Mining Corporation

Signature of Aurora II Mining Corporation Company official:

_____

Please print:

Name: _____

Title: _____

Date: _____

ATTACHMENT

Terms and Conditions

This letter and the attached Terms and Conditions set forth the rights and responsibilities of the parties with respect to the Services. The attachment is an integral part of this agreement.

The laws of the state of Texas shall govern this contract. The federal or state courts of the state of Texas shall have exclusive jurisdiction of any claims arising out of this engagement.

———- Detailed Terms and Conditions omitted

Example certificate of insurance (business insurance)

Most of your larger clients will want to see evidence of business insurance. This is typically an annual expense. Make sure you avoid buying more insurance than you need. If the client has some special safety or security need that does not apply to you, ask to be excluded from the insurance requirement. Riders for transportation of dangerous chemicals, special medical liabilities, etc. can be expensive and provide no value to the client if not relevant to your assignment.

Following is a redacted certificate of insurance showing that at the time of the engagement ICCM had professional liability insurance of $1,000,000. Going forward, the coverage required will likely be multiples of this amount.

Bill Yarberry, CPA

CERTIFICATE OF INSURANCE

PRODUCER	THIS CERTIFICATE IS ISSUED AS A MATTER OF INFORMATION ONLY AND CONFERS NO RIGHTS UPON THE CERTIFICATE HOLDER. THIS CERTIFICATE DOES NOT AMEND, EXTEND OR ALTER THE COVERAGE AFFORDED BY THE POLICIES BELOW.
Houston TX 77098	**COMPANIES AFFORDING COVERAGE**
INSURED ICCM CONSULTING, LLC	COMPANY A
	COMPANY B
	COMPANY C
	COMPANY D

COVERAGES

THIS IS TO CERTIFY THAT THE POLICIES OF INSURANCE LISTED BELOW HAVE BEEN ISSUED TO THE INSURED NAMED ABOVE FOR THE POLICY PERIOD INDICATED. NOTWITHSTANDING ANY REQUIREMENT, TERM OR CONDITION OF ANY CONTRACT OR OTHER DOCUMENT WITH RESPECT TO WHICH THIS CERTIFICATE MAY BE ISSUED OR MAY PERTAIN, THE INSURANCE AFFORDED BY THE POLICIES DESCRIBED HEREIN IS SUBJECT TO ALL THE TERMS, EXCLUSIONS AND CONDITIONS OF SUCH POLICIES. LIMITS SHOWN MAY BEEN REDUCED BY PAID CLAIMS

CO LTR	TYPE OF INSURANCE	POLICY NUMBER	POLICY EFFECTIVE DATE (MM/DD/YY)	POLICY EXPIRATION DATE (MM/DD/YY)	LIMITS	
	GENERAL LIABILITY ☐ COMMERCIAL GENERAL LIABILITY ☐ CLAIMS MADE ☐ OCCUR ☐ OWNER'S & CONT PROT ☐ ☐				GENERAL AGGREGATE PRODUCTS-COMP/OP AGG PERSONAL & ADV INJURY EACH OCCURRENCE FIRE DAMAGE (Any one fire) MED EXP (Any one person)	$ $ $ $ $ $
	AUTOMOBILE LIABILITY ☐ ANY AUTO ☐ ALL OWNED AUTOS ☐ SCHEDULED AUTOS ☐ HIRED AUTOS ☐ NON-OWNED AUTOS ☐				COMBINED SINGLE LIMIT BODILY INJURY (Per person) BODILY INJURY (Per accident) PROPERTY DAMAGE	$ $ $ $
	GARAGE LIABILITY ☐ ANY AUTO ☐ ☐				AUTO ONLY - EA ACCIDENT OTHER THAN AUTO ONLY EACH ACCIDENT AGGREGATE	$ $ $
	EXCESS LIABILITY				EACH OCCURRENCE	$
	☐ ANY AUTO ☐ ALL OWNED AUTOS ☐ SCHEDULED AUTOS ☐ HIRED AUTOS ☐ NON-OWNED AUTOS ☐				COMBINED SINGLE LIMIT BODILY INJURY (Per person) BODILY INJURY (Per accident) PROPERTY DAMAGE	$ $ $ $
	GARAGE LIABILITY ☐ ANY AUTO ☐ ☐				AUTO ONLY - EA ACCIDENT OTHER THAN AUTO ONLY EACH ACCIDENT AGGREGATE	$ $ $
	EXCESS LIABILITY ☐ UMBRELLA FORM ☐ OTHER THAN UMBRELLA FORM				EACH OCCURRENCE AGGREGATE	$ $
	WORKERS COMPENSATION AND EMPLOYER'S LIABILITY THE PROPRIETOR/ PARTNERS/EXECUTIVE ☐ INCL OFFICERS ARE ☐ EXCL				☐ STATUTORY LIMIT EACH ACCIDENT DISEASE - POLICY LIMIT DISEASE - EACH EMPLOYEE	$ $ $
A	**OTHER** PROFESSIONAL LIABILITY- CLAIMS MADE	ECN00044830901			AGGREGATE EACH CLAIM	$1,000,000 $1,000,000

DESCRIPTION OF OPERATIONS/LOCATIONS/VEHICLES/SPECIAL ITEMS EFF: INCEPTION

CERTIFICATE HOLDER	CANCELLATION
	SHOULD ANY OF THE ABOVE DESCRIBED POLICIES BE CANCELLED BEFORE THE EXPIRATION DATE THEREOF, THE ISSUING COMPANY WILL ENDEAVOR TO MAIL ___ DAYS WRITTEN NOTICE TO THE CERTIFICATE HOLDER NAMED TO THE LEFT, BUT FAILURE TO MAIL SUCH NOTICE SHALL IMPOSE NO OBLIGATION OR LIABILITY OF ANY KIND UPON THE COMPANY, ITS AGENTS OR REPRESENTATIVES
*** Client Name and Address Here ***	AUTHORIZED REPRESENTATIVE

Example invoice

ICCM Consulting, LLC
William A. Yarberry, Jr., Principal Consultant
xxxx
Kingwood, TX 77325-6398
Phone (713) 555-6275

INVOICE

INVOICE # 8245-3877

Date: 01-24-18

Bill To:
xxx
Vice President
xxx
xxx
Houston, Texas 77064

Quantity	Description	Hourly Rate	Total	Signed by:
67.00	Wireless communications analytics (Temp Labor 59.98.780.0.81191.0)	$135.00	$9,045.00	xxxxx
4.50	Efficiency Analysis (Temp Labor 59.98.889.0.81191.0)	$135.00	$607.50	xxxxx
39.00	IT Governance Consulting (Temp Labor 59.01.880.0.81191.0)	$135.00	$5,265.00	xxxxx
	Total IT Charges		$ 14,917.50	
	Invoice Total		$ 14,917.50	
			Payment Due	

Remit to: ICCM Consulting, LLC
                 xxxxx
                 Kingwood, TX 77325-6398

Payment terms: Net 7 days after receipt of invoice.

Please reference the
invoice number listed
above on your
payment.

If you have any questions concerning this invoice, please contact Bill Yarberry, 713-555-6275
** Your Business Is Appreciated **

Formal and informal letters of recommendation

Ask for a recommendation at the end of a successful engagement. It need not be formal. Some potential clients will ask for referrals, and RFPs (requests for proposal) often require them. The two recommendations below came from firms of different sizes and industries.

Informal:

RE: Thanks for your business

FROM:

TO: William Yarberry

CC:

Bill,

Thanks for all your hard work on this. I know who I'm calling when something similar rolls around.

Regards,

Performance Manager

From: William Yarberry [mailto:byarberry@iccmconsulting.net]
To:
Cc:
Subject: Thanks for your business

Gentlemen,

I got my last check. Thanks so much for the business. I hope is satisfied with the responses, even though a few required clarification.

Best regards,

Bill

Formal:

To Whom It May Concern:

I am pleased to recommend the services of ICCM Consulting to you. During the last five years, *ICCM* Consulting, under the leadership of Bill Yarberry, has provided my firm with highly satisfactory IT governance, Sarbanes-Oxley and general analytical services. ICCM assisted in the development of our policies and procedures documents, our IT control framework, and has successfully guided us through Sarbanes-Oxley compliance each year since 2004.

In addition, ICCM has provided excellent staff for a variety of projects, including a major telecommunications implementation (both voice and WAN), IT data archiving for a system we put into retirement and specialty projects such as an IT security design review.

On a personal note, Bill Yarberry performs his duties with good professional judgment and continues to maintain a friendly relationship with my staff and other professionals. I am happy to recommend ICCM and Bill in particular.

Please feel free to contact me should you have further questions.

Sincerely,

Miscellaneous ideas to improve your effectiveness and efficiency

There is no single, silver bullet that will enable you to get more done, develop new relationships, or remember details about multiple clients. Instead, it is the summation of many small habits, practiced regularly, that builds your success as a consultant. Here are some random suggestions—pick those that make sense for you.

- Carry a blank notebook in your car. Don't wait too long to pull over after a lengthy cell phone conversation and record critical details.
- Use your commute time effectively. Listen to eBooks, business podcasts, or business news. Being broadly educated is part of the consultant image.
- Never go more than a week without improving at least one skill. Do you know how to run an Excel pivot table? Have you added the latest aero-visco-elasticity options to your standard aeronautics engineering template? Can you send a client a large file using a service like Dropbox? Each skill will have a different set of tools but they all change, and quickly. An hour of learning time pays long dividends.
- Never get so busy that you can't spend five minutes with the people you are close to. Stability in your personal life is part of the expected "good-person" image of a reliable consultant.
- Spend time with people. Lunches, local conferences, trade shows, and other venues are important for exposure to new ideas and chance contacts that could turn into future business.
- Be a fanatic about your contact list. Add notes about your meetings, their interests, needs, and even funny stories. Consulting is a long-term business. If you can recall a story from five years ago about something clever the client's child or dog did, then you have passed through an important hoop.
- Even when you are busy, force yourself to spend a few minutes every day searching the Internet for new developments in your area of expertise.
- Your car can be modest or even old, but never let it get so junked up that you cannot volunteer to take an individual or group to lunch. Raking out twenty empty water bottles so they can sit down does not make a good impression.
- Never, ever crush your client's spirit. Dale Carnegie, as hokey as he now sounds, understood clearly that people need self-esteem to survive. If the client's boat is twelve feet long and yours is twenty feet long, great. Just don't mention it to the client. If your client tells you about Ray Kurzweil's latest insight into artificial intelligence, listen carefully, contribute if you can, but do not remark that it is old news.

- Avoid discussions or comments related to politics, religion or sex. It is tempting when surrounded by like-minded people to chat about such edgy topics. Don't do it.
- Check your invoice thoroughly before submitting it. I've seen consultants who have soured their relationship with the client due to sloppy arithmetic on invoicing. Errors there arouse instant suspicion. Submitting a duplicate invoice is like spitting in the client's coffee and saying "Oh, sorry, you like cream don't you?"
- Never delete anything. Some efficiency "experts" will tell you to do electronic housekeeping by deleting files that you are sure you'll never need again. Who can be that smart or see that far into the future? I've had clients ask me for their files from five years back. Backup is cheap; a terabyte external drive is around $100. Create a subdirectory called "old stuff prior to 2016" to store historical files. Get an online backup service like Carbonite for $10 a month.
- Ensure that any subcontractors physically sign a document indicating that they understand they are not an employee and will not receive any benefits, including unemployment. Put the terms in **LARGE, BOLD, AND CAPITALIZED** print so there is no way the subcontractor can later claim that the information was buried in fine print. The last thing you want is to spend time working with your state workforce office to explain why the individual was not an employee. One subcontractor I used for some clerical work listed "ICCM Consulting" as her last employer. For quite a while the Texas Workforce Commission representative was on my cell phone speed dial.
- Listen to your inner voice. Your subconscious is powerful and smart. It figures out what is important long before your conscious mind does. However, it cannot talk. The bad, gnawing feeling you have sometimes may be your subconscious "shouting" in the only way it can. When you are anxious and upset about something going on in your business, try to relax, listen and interpret the message[14]. It could be vital to your success.
- Welcome change. Massive changes in the next decades will test earth's ability to adapt. As the apex species of the planet, we are obligated to change our mindset continually, both for business and survival itself. So embrace the new. Learning, fifty-two weeks out of the year, is the price of admission.

---

[14] Classic example of how the subconscious mind communicates: The famous German chemist, Friedrich August Kekulé, had been struggling for months to identify the structure of the organic chemical benzene. He fell asleep in front of the fire and dreamed about snakes dancing in the flames. Then suddenly each snake bit another snake on its tail so that together they formed a ring. This was the critical insight that allowed him to deduce the molecule's circular structure.

Bill Yarberry, CPA

Acknowledgements

#1 – My wife Carol: Her common-sense observations and recommendations helped keep the book focused and relevant. I appreciate her many re-readings and support during the writing. She has always been my first line of defence against lazy thought or unclear references, in this and all my previous books.

#2 – My editor, Cyndy Brown: I thought I would get feedback on a few miscellaneous grammar errors when I asked Cyndy for a review. Instead, I received the education I wish I'd had years ago. She suggested dozens of changes to the original manuscript. Her recommendations not only eliminated many errors but also led me to rethink some of the sections. Lesson learned: never underestimate the value of a deeply experienced professional editor.

#3 – Fellow entrepreneur, James Davis: The final review of any book answers the question – does this make sense? Is it plausible? Is it practical?   James provided invaluable feedback based on his own experience. He made me think through some of my assumptions and provided new perspectives. Who really knows their unconscious biases until an experienced, independent observer points them out?

Dedication

To my son Will and my daughter Libby. Thank you for blessing our lives. Your mother and I are proud of what you have accomplished, what you are doing now, and the many contributions you will make in the future. You both serve as exemplary models of the "good person" persona I mention in this book.

* * *

PERMISSION AND DISCLAIMER

Made in the USA
Middletown, DE
27 July 2018